Songs of Praise
A Lent and Easter Companion

For Liz

We would like to thank all who have given us permission to include extracts in this book, as indicated on the list below. Every effort has been made to trace and acknowledge copyright holders. We apologize for any inadvertent errors or omissions.

Text Acknowledgments

pp. 12–13, 33, 46, 52–53, 57–58, 63–64, 78, 98, 102, 104–105: From Revised English Bible © Oxford University Press and Cambridge University Press 1989.

p. 19: 'He who would valiant be' by Percy Dearmer, after John Bunyan. Used with permission.

p. 38: Scripture quotation taken from the Holy Bible, New International Version, copyright © 1973, 1978, 1984 International Bible Society. Used by permission of Zondervan and Hodder & Stoughton Limited. All rights reserved. The 'NIV' and 'New International Version' trademarks are registered in the United States Patent and Trademark Office by International Bible Society. Use of either trademark requires the permission of International Bible Society. UK trademark number 1448790.

p. 38: Extract taken from the song 'The Father's Song' by Matt Redman copyright © 2000 Thankyou Music. Adm. by worshiptogether.com songs excl. UK & Europe, adm. by Kingsway Music. tym@kingsway.co.uk. Used by permission.

p. 40: Extract taken from 'The Donkey' by G.K. Chesterton. Used by permission of A.P. Watt Limited on behalf of the Royal Literary Fund.

p. 45: Extract taken from the song 'Meekness and Majesty' by Graham Kendrick copyright © 1986 ThankyouMusic. Adm. by worshiptogether.com songs excl. UK & Europe, adm. by Kingsway Music. tym@kingsway.co.uk. Used by permission.

p. 74: 'The Paradox' from *A Trophy of Arms* by Ruth Pitter, published by The Cresset Press, 1936.

p. 82: 'Lord of the Dance' by Sydney Carter. © Copyright 1963 Stainer & Bell Ltd, London, England.

p. 106: 'Brother, let me be your servant' by Richard Gillard © Copyright 1977 Scripture in Song (a div. of Integrity Music)/Sovereign Music UK, P.O. Box 356, Leighton Buzzard, LU7 3WP. Reproduced by permission.

p. 112 and jacket flap: 'Now the green blade riseth,' words by J.M.C. Crum (1872–1958) from *The Oxford Book of Carols* © Oxford University Press 1928. Reproduced by permission.

Picture Acknowledgments

All pictures by **Andrew Barr** except as indicated below.

AKG – Images: pp. 39, 75 (Erich Lessing), 104.

BBC/Ronald Grant Archive: p. 58.

Corbis UK Ltd.: pp. 11 (Francis G. Mayer), 16 (Jim Winkley; Ecoscene), 30–31 (Hubert Stadler), 68 and 100–101 (Hulton-Deutsch Collection), 90–91 (Adam Woolfitt).

Illustrated London News: p. 93.

Lion Publishing: pp. 8–9, 80.

Press Association: p. 54 (Johnny Green).

Rex Features: p. 19 (Ian Bradshaw).

Science Photo Library: pp. 60–61 (Art Wolfe).

Picture research courtesy of Zooid Pictures Limited.

Songs of Praise

A LENT AND EASTER COMPANION

ANDREW BARR

A LION BOOK

Published by
Lion Publishing plc
Mayfield House, 256 Banbury Road,
Oxford OX2 7DH, England
www.lion-publishing.co.uk
ISBN 0 7459 5127 9

First edition 2004
10 9 8 7 6 5 4 3 2 1 0

Typeset in 11/14 Berkeley OldStyle Book BT
Printed and bound in Singapore

Contents

● ● ● ● ● ● ● ● ● ● ● ● ● ●

Preface

• • • • • • • • • • • • •

The three days of storm ended in the night,
and with the wild weather there departed from
the Cruives something which had weighed on
Dickson's spirits since he first saw the place.
Monday saw the return of the sun and the bland
airs of spring. Beyond the blue of the yet restless
waters rose dim mountains tipped with snow.
Nesting birds were busy on the Laver banks
and in the Huntingtower thickets: the village
smoked peacefully to the clear skies. Assuredly,
thought Dickson, there had come a mighty
change in the countryside, and he meditated
a future discourse to the Literary Society of the
Guthrie Memorial Kirk on 'Natural Beauty in
Relation to the Mind of Man'.

FROM *HUNTINGTOWER* BY JOHN BUCHAN (1875–1940)

I grew up on John Buchan's adventure stories. They stimulated my imagination on dark nights as my brother and I listened to the radio in the 1950s, the great days of BBC Radio Drama. The opening of the last chapter of *Huntingtower* is classic Buchan, with the hero, Dickson McCunn, not only concluding a battle against the wild Scots landscape and its unpredictable weather, but also helping to thwart invading evildoers. Buchan used familiar people and places to create strange and exciting plots.

I have grown out of *Boys' Own* adventure stories, but I still enjoy Buchan's scene-setting. Many of *Huntingtower*'s chapters begin with the dawn of a new day so, even though I don't have to deliver a discourse on 'Natural Beauty in Relation to the Mind of Man', my preface to this *Songs of Praise: A Lent and Easter Companion* begins at dawn -- on Easter Day, as I set out to greet the sunrise on a spring morning, listening to Radio 4's *Prayer for the Day* on the car radio.

Near its end, the A68 from Darlington to Edinburgh comes out of the wooded hills of Midlothian above the village of Cousland. On the best of days, days like today, when weeks of storms have vanished in the night, a panoramic view of Edinburgh, the Firth of Forth and the distant Highlands is crystal clear in the stillness. Surely, in the great Scots storyteller's words, 'a mighty change has come'.

For most of us, for most of life, 'a mighty change' seems unlikely. But small, imperceptible changes happen every day, whether we notice them or not, and for us, as for the hero of *Huntingtower*, the natural world can sometimes play a big and unexpected part in helping us notice them. This book is the story of many journeys as I have tried to discover and capture how it is that the days of Lent and Passiontide and Easter, however familiar, however often we repeat the process year by year, can still bring about both small and mighty changes.

On my travels, the one companion that I never leave home without is my camera. The ageing, now rather battered, Olympus OM2 has endured every sort of climate and together with Fuji 800ASA film has achieved many modern miracles, including capturing moments of *Songs of Praise* recordings in near darkness. It has become my record of the many faces of Britain, never the same on any two days, where the programmes are made.

Even if the changes we do see are small rather than mighty, they can still be profound. One Sunday afternoon after Easter, on a lengthy motorway journey from Scotland, the service area where I stopped was overflowing with customers. In the full and featureless car park, a vacated space was like heaven's gateway, and like many other travellers, I was there in search of a

cash machine. Rest or refreshment seemed unlikely to be on offer as people rushed in and out of the swing doors. Some had mobile telephones clamped to their ears, others tried to organize overtired and over-stimulated children, while a middle-aged woman barely concealed her impatience with the slowness of her elderly mother who was creeping cautiously towards the Ladies on her Zimmer. It all seemed grimly hopeless, until two people passed by, apparently being tugged along by a carpet, or, as it turned out, a big mongrel dog. He had clearly been cooped up in the family saloon far too long and was rushing headlong towards some trees. Out of pure nosiness and a tendency to like dogs, I followed them, weaving through the cars, and

I was seemingly miraculously led into a new world.
Beyond the dusty, dirty car park lay a woodland carpeted
with bluebells, where trees absorbed the traffic noise but
not the evening birdsong.

I heard the voice of Jesus say,
'Come unto me and rest;
lay down, thou weary one, lay down
thy head upon my breast.'
I came to Jesus as I was,
weary, and worn, and sad;
I found in him a resting-place,
and he has made me glad.

H. BONAR (1808–89)

When Sir Harry Secombe and I
walked into another woodland,
in Hampshire, in March 1991,
we truly saw 'a mighty change'.
Walking towards us came Jenny
Rees Larcombe, whom we had last seen at the
Christian Healing Centre at Burrswood in Kent, in
great pain and apparently wheelchair-bound for life.
As a Christian, Jenny believed that through prayer she
could be healed. And now, there she was, walking towards us.

The change was great for her, she told Sir Harry, but strangely, quite
difficult for some of the many people who had looked after her for all
the years she had been dependent on her chair. She was keen to show
us she could even jog, but our own faith did not extend to allowing her
to demonstrate this to the camera.

I heard the voice of Jesus say,
'I am this dark world's light;
look unto me, thy morn shall rise,
and all thy day be bright.'
I looked to Jesus, and I found
in him my star, my sun;
and in that light of life I'll walk,
till travelling days are done.

H. BONAR

In its forty years' history, *Songs of Praise* has included many other such dramatic moments in people's lives. Mostly, however, as hundreds of people have told us their stories of faith, they have been describing the daily round of small changes, of courageous journeys, of hopes raised and hopes dashed as Lent and Easter come and go. Year by year, week by week, they have created a mighty patchwork of stories celebrating Christian faith.

This *Songs of Praise: A Lent and Easter Companion* describes and celebrates some of their journeys, as well as journeys in my own life in broadcasting, which have taken me to Bosnia, to Birmingham and nearly to the North Pole. It looks back at past programmes that have gone through the six weeks of Lent to Easter and beyond, and it describes the continuing story of a series that still draws millions of viewers, including me, to the television every Sunday evening.

Once again, Kathleen Frew and my wife, Liz, have typed and criticized and stopped me from rambling on too much; Morag Reeve and Nick Rous, Commissioning Editor and Senior Designer at Lion Publishing, have trusted me to return home eventually with a book, and I am grateful for all their continuing support, as I am to the present *Songs of Praise* team, led by Hugh Faupel and Michael Wakelin.

LENT

Temptation of Christ on the Mountain by Duccio di Buoninsegna (c. 1308–11)

chapter one

The Devil You Know

• • • • • • • • • • • • •

Jesus was then led by the Spirit into the wilderness, to be tempted by the devil. For forty days and nights he fasted, and at the end of them he was famished. The tempter approached him and said, 'If you are the Son of God, tell these stones to become bread.' Jesus answered, 'Scripture says, "Man is not to live on bread alone, but on every word that comes from the mouth of God."'

The devil then took him to the Holy City and set him on the parapet of the temple. 'If you are the Son of God,' he said, 'throw yourself down; for scripture says, "He will put his angels in charge of you, and they will support you in their arms, for fear you should strike your foot against a stone."' Jesus answered him, 'Scripture also says, "You are not to put the Lord your God to the test."'

The devil took him next to a very high mountain, and showed him all the kingdoms of the world in their glory. 'All these,' he said, 'I will give you, if you will only fall down and do me homage.' But Jesus said, 'Out of my sight, Satan! Scripture says, "You shall do homage to

the Lord your God and worship him alone." '
  Then the devil left him; and angels came and
attended to his needs.

MATTHEW 4:1–11

'Oh Andy! Couldn't you give up moaning for Lent?'
     My mother was exasperated as she turned to me from the sink,
     her hands plunged in a washing-up bowl full of suds. I was in
familiar pose, leaning against my favourite pulpit, the fridge, repeating my
litany of all the woes in my life, while my mother worked her way through
the daily round of chores in our labour-intensive kitchen. Even now, nearly
fifty years on, the memory still induces a feeling of guilt in me.

   Although it was the spring half-term, that last day of school had
become for me one of unparalleled tragedy, and I needed to know why
the world was so unfair. Bullying? Punishment? Lost the football match?
Not a bit of it. As I was completing the walk home, all the joy of half-term
freedom had turned to bitter disappointment as I got the first whiff of my
favourite smell: tar. Our dull-grey avenue had been completely resurfaced,
and I had missed the excitement of the decade – the technicolour invasion
of steam-shrouded tar boilers and clanking road rollers. Now there was
nothing left except smart white chippings and the tantalizing smell of
the glistening tar. I might as well have missed a total eclipse of the sun.

   I can't remember how I responded to my mother's plea at the time,
but it was uncharacteristic of her to use religion to cope with my pathetic
protests against the unfairness of life. Mostly I picture her, between
cigarettes, singing at the sink: *'I'll be loving you: always; with a love that's true:*
always.' That usually started up when *Housewives' Choice* on the BBC Light
Programme ended and the radio was smartly switched off after no more
than the first two notes of a hymn on *Five to Ten*, the brief weekday religious
broadcast that followed.

My mother's love for her family was expressed in what she did and only very rarely in words, but the memory of her humming that tune and singing those words as she coped with a long and distressing illness says more to me now about courage and love than anything she might have said.

We didn't really 'do God' in our family, although we started regimes of going to church many times. New leaves were regularly turned over so, in a way, my first understanding of Lent was that it was an all-year event. We were forever trying to give up our respective bad habits and resist all the daily temptations of life in the South London suburbs. Though with sweets rationed until I was eleven, there wasn't much chance to either practise or resist the sin of gluttony.

Every spring, however, our year-round Lent was suspended and we prepared for our Easter break. Our house was almost unheated, we had no mod-cons, the furniture was old and shabby and the decor tired, but no expense was spared when we left home for our holidays. We would travel through the night to wake to the loud and disorganized clanging of cathedral bells celebrating Easter in the south of France or to eat cream cakes on Easter Day surrounded by German families at a lakeside restaurant in the Black Forest. We once betrayed our Anglo-Saxon attitudes when the Easter greetings warmly offered to us in Italian by a café owner in Milan were mistaken for the bill. My father began proffering lire notes, muttering his only words of Italian 'Scusi! Scusi!' and everybody in the café looked so shocked that we hastily scrambled out of the premises.

I first read the stories of Jesus and his disciples in the strip cartoons in the *Eagle* comic, although both Jeremy, my younger brother, and I would turn rather more eagerly to the heroic space exploits of Colonel Dan Dare, ever beating his bright green adversary, the Mekon. But even to us, the Mekon seemed too ridiculous to be really frightening, so it was through *Flook*, the cartoon in the *Daily Mail,* that we were first introduced to real evil. Moses Maggot, a small bald-headed man in dark glasses, who looked remarkably like many of our neighbours, constantly pursued a little fair-haired boy called Rufus and his peculiar, curly-haired pal with trotters, Flook. Maggot's evil-doings were centred on a small hut that looked exactly like our own potting shed, so fear of its dark interior became my excuse never to go in and collect spades and hoes to help out in the garden. Through my silly, childish view of the world, the devil had managed to get to me in the form of Moses Maggot, while Jesus was just another figure in a comic, who I usually neglected and always let down.

Sent away to boarding school, far away from my kitchen pulpit and the potting shed, I had to learn to look after myself. I was at my happiest when I went alone into 'the wilderness'. Rugby School nearly fifty years ago was awash with rules and regulations that applied inside the school grounds, but once outside, even the most junior schoolboy could roam freely. Nearby was real countryside as I had never before experienced it, and several times a week I made a silent retreat.

In the Lent term, when the ground was too hard for hockey, I would walk rapidly past the huge sports fields and on up to the crossroads where a clump of huge bare-branched trees was filled with welcoming rooks. Here began Onley Lane, its name board appropriately prefaced with an extra 'L'. This was my private world. Dropping downhill, the road was soon in a shallow valley where Warwickshire stretched into distant Oxfordshire. No cars intruded on my silent pilgrimage, but just occasionally huge steam-hauled coal trains would dash across the landscape on the high embankment carrying the old Great Central Railway to London. Further on, seen only by silently cud-chewing cows, I reached my safe haven – the canal.

In the book *Narrow Boat*, one of the very few books my father ever allowed my brother or me to take down from his precious bookshelves and read for ourselves, L.T.C. Rolt described a journey on Britain's canals in the last year before the Second World War. Each night he tied up somewhere new and slept snug, cosy and safe in the tiny cabin of 'Cressy', his converted working barge. In the cold spring of 1939, he reached my 1956 safe haven, on the Oxford Canal near Rugby:

Dusk found us crossing a wilderness of flat scrub pasture-land, which, on referring to my map, I found to be the edge of Dunsmore Heath, and it was in this desolate place, under the meagre shelter of a row of stunted thorn bushes, that we moored for the night in a rising gale. It blew so hard overnight that 'Cressy' uprooted both her mooring spikes and drifted astern for over two hundred yards, fortunately without swinging across the channel or doing any damage.

FROM *NARROW BOAT* BY L.T.C. ROLT

I was feeling lost in my own 'desolate place', a big, public-school community, where it was possible to be lonely but never alone. Coming to

my 'wilderness', sitting by the canal, pretending that I too had a little canal boat and a secure cabin, I discovered the private world of my imagination, which has been my defence ever since. Whenever I could, I made for the humpback bridge, under which weather-beaten pairs of laden working boats passed south to Oxford. The motor barge would come first, towing behind her on a long rope the 'butty' barge with its tiny cabin and huge ram's head rudder post. Although by the 1950s the canal boats had been nationalized, the man at the helm of the motor and his wife at the rudder of the 'butty' could have come straight out of Victorian England. They proudly displayed their own individualism in the brightly coloured pails and utensils of their private world.

Back at school, I went to a course of Lent lectures, chiefly because most of the other boys didn't go. I don't recall a word of the lectures, but I shall never forget a sentence that was spoken in the school chapel one morning that Lent. The chapel was as impressive as a cathedral. To the left was the high altar under which the famous Dr Arnold was buried, while to the right sat my own headmaster, Sir Arthur Fforde, a small dark figure almost invisible, surrounded by dark wainscoting. Even shown in a recent *Songs of Praise* from Rugby, the chapel still inspires awe in me. That morning I was sitting in the wrong pew. As ever, I was aware of the misdemeanour but unable to understand the rule that would tell me where I ought to be.

The voice that introduced God to me that morning simply asked each one of us in the chapel to pray for the bishop of Coventry, who was very ill. The way the invisible speaker put it, each one of us could make a difference, not through any dutiful behaviour, but by simply praying. I suddenly thought, as long as I told nobody what I was doing, God and I, in private, together, would make the difference.

As Lent turned into Holy Week, the school broke up for the Easter holiday. I stayed behind in the school sanatorium, having caught a throat bug, which developed into nephritis, an awkward and very painful complication. By Easter Day 1956, I was in the greatest pain I have ever experienced.

As it passed, the comfort I slowly began to feel came less from medicine than from drawing paper. Deprived of walks into my 'wilderness', I could at least try to draw and paint it. One by one, the school chaplains came to jolly me along, each promising eventual release. But it was the totally unexpected and inexplicable appearance at my bedside of the head of the art department, Mr Talbot Kelly, a famous bird painter, that turned my first real Lent into my first real Easter. He sat on the bed and looked at my drawings of the canal. They were full of detail, but as he gently indicated, I had no concept of perspective. In a couple of strokes of a pencil, he transformed my two-dimensional world into a three-dimensional world. My imagination was set free. Now, not only would my drawings show others how the world looked through my eyes, but for the first time I began to see how the world looked through other people's eyes. Even through my mother's, as she patiently listened to her thin, gloomy son moaning as he leaned against the fridge.

Just recently, through the repeat of the wonderful BBC TWO series *The Great War*, I saw for the first time Talbot Kelly's own view of the world. He had been in the trenches in France, and in this series, recorded in 1963, he recalled the sights and smells of death in such vivid detail that he eventually fell silent mid-sentence. One Easter holiday afternoon in 1956, in the school sanatorium, he used his skill and his experience to transform my loneliness and pain into something that has kept me going ever since.

Noel Vincent, a former *Songs of Praise* producer and recently retired Canon Chancellor of Liverpool's Anglican cathedral, remembers that he too was unprepared for boarding-school life. But he looks back with gratitude to the night when, as he wept at the prospect of being sent away from home the next day, his normally uncommunicative, rather austere father sat on his bed and solemnly sang to him John Bunyan's hymn, 'He who would valiant be'.

He who would valiant be
'gainst all disaster,
let him in constancy
follow the Master.
There's no discouragement
shall make him once relent
his first avowed intent
to be a pilgrim.

Who so beset him round
with dismal stories,
do but themselves confound –
his strength the more is.
No foes shall stay his might,
though he with giants fight:
he will make good his right
to be a pilgrim.

Since, Lord, thou dost defend
us with thy Spirit,
we know we at the end
shall life inherit.
Then fancies flee away!
I'll fear not what men say,
I'll labour night and day
to be a pilgrim.

PERCY DEARMER (1867–1936) AFTER JOHN BUNYAN (1628–88)

chapter two

Ashes

● ● ● ● ● ● ● ● ● ● ● ●

That come before the swallow dares, and take
The winds of March with beauty.

FROM *THE WINTER'S TALE* BY WILLIAM SHAKESPEARE (1564–1616)

Shrove Tuesday in Ashby St Ledgers, and the daffs are all in bloom. As
I get older, my car journeys between England and my home in Scotland
become ever more of a meander, and so I break the journey in a peaceful
Northamptonshire village mercifully just out of earshot of the nearby M1
motorway. The pub is almost deserted at lunchtime, and nobody orders
pancakes on the last day before Lenten austerity takes over. Two men chatter
loudly, not confessing their sins in the tradition of 'shriving' which gives this
Tuesday its name, but celebrating what sounds like a plan to celebrate the sure
and certain sin of gluttony. The 'risk-free' business proposition on the table
can apparently lead only to limitless profit and maybe it's because I am sort
of trying not to listen that I never discover what the business actually involves.

The daffodil-lined village street leads past the wonderfully named
'Snoozy Cottage' to the parish church of the Blessed Virgin Mary and
St Leodegarius. It is everything you could hope for in an English village
church. It is adjacent to a famous manor house where four centuries ago
conspirators met to plan the Gunpowder Plot to blow up parliament,
and this Shrove Tuesday, with today's parliamentarians clamouring their
opposing views about an impending war, the door is wide open and a huge
notice 'Pray for peace' is pinned to the church's ancient timbers. Coming in
from bright sunshine, it's even harder than usual to see the wall paintings
that are, as John Betjeman warns visitors reading his Collins Church guide,

'extensive but dim'. There on the west wall, a forgotten artist of the 16th century painted figures to represent Time and Death. Even in their faded, almost ghostly form, they add their eloquently silent commentary to the day's chattering news broadcasts.

In the deep silence of the church, sitting in the old musicians' gallery and looking across to the single-manual organ, my instinctive old *Songs of Praise* director's questions come back: where could I fit four TV cameras in here? The answer in my heyday would have been 'not possible', for at the most perhaps 100 people could fit into the pews, even without all the technical paraphernalia of a traditional *Songs of Praise* Outside Broadcast unit. But while listening apprehensively to news updates of what the pundits claim will be a 'high-tech' war, I have to admit that it is to the worldwide defence industry that TV owes the innovations that can be put to peaceful use in programmes like *Songs of Praise*. Now, high-quality video cameras, originally developed for espionage and small enough to be held in the palm of a hand, can do the work of the old, heavy and cumbersome OB cameras, mounted on trolleys, which were quite capable of falling through an ancient church floor like this one and frequently did so.

In the last few years, *Songs of Praise* has occasionally been following different themes, such as a recent series about marriage and baptism, where an unobtrusive camera allowed viewers to see the christening of Aled Jones's little baby girl, Emilia. Although these themed programmes are more about individuals and ideas than the life of communities, the current directors can now create magic moments with small choirs in these beautiful little ancient churches that were once completely out of bounds to the old, heavy technology directors like me.

St Leodegarius, with its wall paintings and rare Jacobean three-decker pulpit would be my ideal location for a hymn about God's justice and forgiveness. For one thing that has drawn me to this church today is a memory of coming here several years ago. I had called in by chance one Sunday, on another long journey south, just in time for the parish communion. The congregation was small but welcoming, sharing the readings and prayers. But it was the young (or youngish) priest who caught my imagination. Listening to a complex yet beautifully and simply expressed sermon about his own and everyone's need of forgiveness, I was reminded of George Herbert, the seventeenth-century poet who left the privileges of life in the royal court to devote himself to the cure of souls in another tiny country parish just like Ashby St Ledgers.

This priest seemed to have been inspired by the words of one of George Herbert's best-loved hymns:

Come, my Way, my Truth, my Life:
such a Way, as gives us breath:
such a Truth, as ends all strife:
such a Life, as killeth death.

Forgiveness was the theme of *Songs of Praise* from another little-known church, St Barnabas in Jericho, Oxford, where the Reading Phoenix Choir sang one of the nation's favourite hymns, 'Dear Lord and Father of mankind, forgive our foolish ways'. The church, apart from having its own proud history as an Anglo-Catholic church built to serve the poorest part of Victorian Oxford, also played its part in Thomas Hardy's novel, *Jude the Obscure*, where it was called St Silas in Beersheba!

Buildings may offer beauty and sanctuary, but with most episodes of *Songs of Praise*, it is the stories of people that stay longest in my memory. In the *Songs of Praise* about forgiveness, Archbishop Desmond Tutu, former archbishop of Capetown, described the experience of helping the South African nation emerge from decades of apartheid. 'In two years of listening, we have seen how forgiveness has helped us all deal with a very distressing past.'

The programme showed clips of both black and white witnesses telling their stories to the South African Truth and Reconciliation Commission. 'Truth can be disruptive, but also therapeutic and healing,' said Desmond Tutu, 'and one was exhilarated in that yes, we had the capacity for evil, but also the wonderful, wonderful capacity for good.'

An extraordinary scene was shown of a white man crying, remembering his dead wife. 'Did you shoot her?' he asked a very small black boy. 'She was wearing a blue coat.'

'I don't know,' said the boy, who too was in great distress. 'I just pointed my gun at the people – but we are asking you please, please for forgiveness.'

'I forgive you unconditionally, as a Christian, for what you did to me,' replied the white man.

'It is not facile to forgive. It is very difficult, but there is no future without forgiveness,' said Desmond Tutu who, like Nelson Mandela, has his own painful story to tell of suffering, imprisonment and persecution in the days of apartheid. 'Remember, each person remains a child of God and each has the possibility of being good. It is not once a murderer, always a murderer. Otherwise history is closed.'

By the end of my journey home from Ashby St Ledgers to Scotland, it is Ash Wednesday. It is too late to go to church, so Liz and I share our own Ash Wednesday ceremony in the kitchen, based on what each of us can remember from past services. In church, the priest or minister leading the 'Imposition of Ashes' service absolves us of our sins before using ashes to make the sign of the cross on our foreheads as we kneel before the altar. This evening in the kitchen there are just the two of us, as we first break apart two palm crosses that have decorated the grandfather clock in the hall since Palm Sunday last year. The broken pieces go into a bowl we both treasure, edged with the words 'Love, Laugh, Live', then we each write our sins on a piece of paper and place them in the bowl and burn the contents to make our own ashes. This is unduly complicated, because I have lit the match too soon and we can only find one bit of paper in the kitchen so it has to be shared as we scribble our regrets. We carefully don't look at what the other has written.

We begin to wonder if our palm crosses are subject to European Community fire-proof regulations as they do not burn at all readily. If our written confessions were hurried, there is plenty of time now to keep silence as they only very slowly turn to ash.

Liz marks a healthy black cross on my travel-stained face, and I feel different – better. Lent begins with the washing-up of our favourite bowl, which now appears to be indelibly stained with a grey scum from our bonfire. But at least history is not closed.

The Sinner

Lord, how I am all ague, when I seek
What I have treasur'd in my memorie!
Since, if my soul make even with the week,
Each seventh note by right is due to thee.
I finde there quarries of pil'd vanities,
But shreds of holinesse, that dare not venture
To shew their face, since crosse to thy decrees:
There the circumference earth is, heav'n the centre.
In so much dregs the quintessence is small:
The spirit and good extract of my heart
Comes to about the many hundredth part.
Yet, Lord, restore thine image, heare my call:
And though my hard heart scarce to thee can grone,
Remember that thou once didst write in stone.

GEORGE HERBERT (1593–1633)

Wilderness

●●●●●●●●●●●●●●

chapter three

Quasa's wife died this winter of starvation. This
we learnt in the following conversation with him
after dinner:

    Q: – Where's your wife?

    A: – She's disappeared.

    Q: – (Guessing that, as her name is no longer
          mentioned, she is dead). What caused
          her to pass away?

    A: – She was too skinny.

ENTRY IN MY DIARY OF A 1970 FILM TRIP TO THE CANADIAN ARCTIC.

I had never seen a true wilderness before and I was frightened. It was also
my first flight in a single-engine aeroplane, my first – and I hope my last
– not only without a seatbelt but without even a seat. I was wedged in
by film equipment, and later discovered that I was crouching on a box of
live ammunition.

Five thousand feet below was the most inhospitable land I have ever
seen. At first, the black, boulder-strewn ground was punctuated by small
frozen lakes of ice, then the land became hidden under dirty-white snow
and the lakes turned black. Thick clouds obscured the sun, and with no
shadows in the completely featureless, treeless world it was impossible to
tell which way our plane was facing. The noise was deafening. We were on
the way to film some of the world's last nomadic Eskimos, and now we
were lost in the wilderness.

At the furthest extremity of Canada's north-west territory is the region called the Barrens. A little further north is the Arctic Circle. Even further, and almost as close to the North Pole as humans can live all the year round, is Bathhurst Inlet. In 1970, the Inuit Eskimos still preferred a nomadic way of life, hunting herds of wild caribou as they migrated annually across the vast, silent and otherwise empty world. Yet, as our filming trip would reveal, an ancient way of life was about to come to an end.

Our guide, and the subject of the film for which I was the sound recordist, claimed to know the terrain like the back of his hand. Born and bred on the banks of the Clyde, Duncan Pryde had not only chosen the wilderness as home, working for the Hudson's Bay Trading Company, but had even become an elected politician serving a constituency in which his was the only non-Inuit name on the electoral roll.

This was a journey of a lifetime, and I kept a diary, sometimes minute by minute, of our expedition. I was scribbling away nervously when, even on our very first leg of the journey, we were already in trouble.

Wednesday, 3.15 p.m.
I'm firmly wedged-in, but Duncan, swathed in caribou skin, seems restless and keeps peering out. I wish he wouldn't smoke – he's sitting on extra cans of aviation fuel.

4.50 p.m.
John, the pilot, admits we're completely lost. He says that we must try to turn back (whichever way that is), but Duncan wants to go on. The radio compass seems to offer little information and the magnetic compass is equally unreliable so near the North Pole. The pilot endlessly studies a map with almost no detail. I just want to touch the ground and leave the BBC. If God had meant us to fly, he wouldn't have given us railways.

7.20 p.m.
After nearly 5 hours of flying, we land back right where we started on the frozen lake in Yellowknife. Tomorrow we will begin the ordeal all over again!

Saturday – *Flying again at 1,000 feet; speed 90 m.p.h.*
1.35 p.m.
As we left Yellowknife the temperature was –10°C and the forecast bad. Duncan seems to have a hangover, but is as restless as ever. The pilot is smoking a pipe and is more reassuring, which is welcome since we have now discovered his flying certificate was once suspended because he so often got lost.
3.17 p.m.
John, the pilot, suddenly dips the plane. Once again, we have crossed the Arctic Circle. Temperature in the aircraft is 0°C – but I'm sweating.
4.40 p.m.
Rough and wild landing on the pack ice, but I don't care any more. We're there.

'There' was Baychimo, a black cabin that looked as if it was once the setting for a Charlie Chaplin film. Some distance away were remnants of igloos, a smaller hut and a few tents. Many Eskimos seemed to appear from nowhere to greet Duncan.

We all received an incredibly warm welcome and it was made clear that our Inuit hosts wanted us to share everything that they had. So we had the best of their food and shelter, as well as the use of an 18-foot-long shed and a dog-team.

We had our ambitions to make an award-winning film, with shots of our heroic trapper driving the dog team out onto the ice-sea close to the North Pole. But it soon became clear that the reality was that these nomadic people were in deep trouble. Until we arrived, they had been very short of food, because for the first time the caribou had not appeared. The Inuit told us that a new oil pipeline had been built right across the herd's route, just high enough to block their path. To this day, I am not certain if this was really the case, for shortly afterwards, these Eskimos, almost the last nomads in Canada, were coaxed into a settlement to help us make the romantic film of our ignorant preconceptions.

So a pagan way of life, where elders who became senile were shot and

where justice quite literally meant an eye for an eye and a tooth for a tooth, was exchanged for a missionary settlement of money and alcohol. I don't think it was the Eskimos' time of temptation – I think it was ours.

My diary records our succumbing to many temptations in that wilderness, and while God did not lose patience with us, the animal kingdom did. Each day Duncan harnessed the nine-dog team, assisted by our host, Iksik, who to my distress controlled them with a spade handle. Duncan explained that the dogs, while permanently cheerful, were also lazy and disobedient. They had to recognize a human boss and also respect one of their own number chosen to lead the team.

Sunday, 2 p.m.

Hilarious start to the sled journey on the Arctic Sea. We start with a huge jerk and Ian, the cameraman, falls off. I learn the value of the ice anchor, our only brake for the sled, which is operated by throwing it and then falling on it. Thank God, it holds. The team go in ever-decreasing circles and finally plunge into the derelict igloo and begin a huge fight amongst themselves. Now we travel at 1 m.p.h. owing to frequent stops to recover film equipment and mainly having to walk on the sea-ice, which is very exhausting. The silence is eerie. Duncan says the dogs must always be facing away from base otherwise they could take off and abandon us.

Out on the sea, unlike the Barrens, we were in an incredibly beautiful world of brilliant white ice frozen into exotic shapes, and the sky above was a deep, clear blue. For the dogs, our classic film shots of 'man against the elements' were pointless and they didn't like retakes any more than most *Songs of Praise* congregations and choirs normally do.

7.15 p.m.
The director is determined. We must film Duncan building an igloo and then wait to film a shot of him driving off into the arctic sunset.

It takes so long that all four of us have to help. To my surprise, I manage to cut quite a decent ice block, but tempers are frayed. So, unbeknown to us, are the dogs' harnesses. Whether 'boss dog' at the front is aware or not, a dog in the middle has eaten through the harness. Suddenly, the front half of the team are free and wheel round to head confidently home. The disgruntled remnant whirl around and tip our equipment out over a wide area of the ice.

We ended up with a ridiculous shot of half a dog team and finished the day with a long, exhausting walk back to base while the remaining dogs carried our film equipment. Back at the hut and the real world of the Inuit, a small baby was very ill. Duncan tried to radio for help and, as my diary revealed, I realized that we were not filming the real story.

Our last day with the Inuit began badly. Duncan emerged from his hut with a huge trunk, like something from *Treasure Island*. He wanted to take it on the plane back to Yellowknife. At first the pilot said that there was no room. 'OK,' replied Duncan, revealing his tough Clydeside origins, 'I'm not coming back with you; I'll just return with the dog team.' He was serious, even though it would be a 500-mile journey across a territory where people had often simply vanished. With our amiable pilot's poor sense of direction, to go without Duncan sounded like madness to me.

Finally, we took off with both Duncan and the trunk, as the pilot shouted, 'We won't clear the ridge' (which surrounded the bay). Not for the last time, I didn't look, and with the trunk at my back, and the 'brace position' so cheerfully indicated on normal flights being out of the question,

I closed my eyes tightly and began to form a strategy for my future, in the unlikely event that I was to escape from this madness with my life.

We just cleared the ridge, relieved that at the last minute dozens of trays of Cola had been taken off the plane and given to our still-smiling, still hungry, but by now puzzled hosts. I cannot remember whether the cans had any ring-pulls.

Almost unbelievably, my diary records that within ten minutes we were once again lost. When we regained our bearings, we were tempted into a final act of filming madness as a few caribou were spotted near an

alleged fuel dump. We were short of fuel anyway, and we landed. We filmed. Duncan shot and missed. Mightily relieved, I was just climbing back into the plane when Duncan wildly fired his final shot from the door. Six hundred feet away, a caribou fell.

Once again, we trudged off through the deep snow, and we filmed Duncan skinning the dead beast. Then, gingerly and guiltily, I ate my first raw caribou.

Our last temptation in the wilderness was to try to get back to Yellowknife without the hassle of refuelling from the drums and cans at the dump. The diary records that we did take off without extra fuel, and so for the last hour my eyes were glued to the fuel gauge. It hit nought somewhere over the frozen lake outside Yellowknife. The engine cut out. We dropped rather rapidly. When I took my hands away from my ears and opened my eyes, we were jolting wildly across the ice. It might as well have been heaven. Apparently we still had five gallons of fuel left, but I needed to set the fashion, later taken up by Pope John Paul II, of kissing God's good earth.

Duncan laughed and closed *The Art of Survival*, a book he had dug out of his wretched hut. I made for a bath and, for the first time in my life, the hotel's Gideon Bible, with a resolve in future to only ever tell real stories about the real world. That night, I began to conceive a strategy which was to lead me to *Songs of Praise* and 30 years of religious-programme-making.

O Jesus, I have promised
to serve thee to the end;
be thou for ever near me,
my master and my friend:
I shall not fear the battle
if thou art by my side,
nor wander from the pathway
if thou wilt be my guide.

J.E. BODE (1816–74)

New Singers, New Songs

chapter four

Sing a new song to the Lord.
Sing to the Lord, all the earth.
Sing to the Lord and bless his name;
day by day proclaim his victory.
Declare his glory among the nations,
his marvellous deeds to every people.

PSALM 96:1–3

Aled Jones is smiling the smile that lights up *Songs of Praise*. If I had to name the human being who most resembles my favourite character in Lewis Caroll's *Alice in Wonderland*, the Cheshire Cat, it would be Aled. Whether he is in a medieval cathedral or on the draughty showground of the Greenbelt Festival, the first thing you notice, and the impression that remains with you after he has gone, is his warm smile. It will certainly be needed during the recording this evening, when after a long day's non-stop rehearsal we will be asked to stand and sing – for a third time – 'Praise, my soul, the King of heaven'.

Today, Aled Jones and *Songs of Praise* have come to Birmingham, to celebrate the newest generation of choristers, the young singers taking part in a festival of school choirs. In the glittering surroundings of one of the newest and finest concert halls in Britain, Birmingham's Symphony Hall, Britain's junior and senior school choirs have entered a competition. The two winning choirs are to be chosen by a panel of judges.

Aled is definitely not in the know, but during the final preparations, while the six shortlisted choirs rehearse with the television cameras, he keeps the children on tenterhooks, making jokes and pretending to fumble with the 'winning' envelopes. 'And the winner is…' Pins can be heard dropping in the vast hall; all the singers are standing stock-still. 'The winner is… Michael Wakelin!' (The *Songs of Praise* series producer, sitting on his own out in the stalls.) A mixture of laughter and groans comes from the singers as they realize that they will still have to wait until the night for the real thing.

Since early morning, hundreds of children and young people from the six shortlisted choirs, three junior and three senior, who have travelled from as far afield as Devon, and Bangor in Northern Ireland, have been taking over Symphony Hall. One by one they have been shown in to the high security surroundings of Hall 8 to perform for the judges. Carrie Grant, singer and music coach from *Fame Academy*, Malcolm Archer, master of music at Wells Cathedral and Pete Waterman, pop music producer and celebrity judge for *Pop Idol*, make up the formidable judging team.

After performing for the judges, the young singers all seem brimming with confidence as they rehearse for the *Songs of Praise* recording that evening. Perhaps it is because they know that the die is cast. They have done their best for the competition, and now all they have to do is perform in front of television cameras for a few million viewers…

Each choir had chosen one traditional hymn and one contemporary Christian song for the competition, and had posted their own audio tape recordings to the BBC some weeks previously. Mark Warburton, working for *Songs of Praise*, did not have any difficulty in persuading the rest of the production team to listen to all the entries as they came in, setting up speakers in every corner of the religious broadcasting offices in Manchester. The team then worked through a careful selection process, rather like the early rounds of the World Cup. Their lunchtime concerts created a shortlist of 12 choirs, and then Mark set off with a tiny hi-tech video camera to film them at school.

Hilary Mason, conductor of the 70-strong Maltman's Green Primary School Choir, chose 'The Father's Song' by Matt Redman. This is a beautiful but demanding song, which they began with a piano introduction over which three solo voices spoke verses from the prophecy of Zephaniah in the Bible. It took split-second timing and, to my ears, faith, for Amy, Charley and Nikki to take their cues from each other.

Mrs Mason tells me that the choir has talked a lot about these verses of scripture. 'The song immediately appealed to them when we first sang it. They liked the theme that whoever, whatever or wherever, God loves you. They also liked the idea that with so many people watching *Songs of Praise*, their song could make a difference.'

As I listen to the young voices, I am reminded of the day when I was still at school, when we were asked to pray for a sick person because it could 'make a difference'. On that spring morning in 1956, I had seen God in a new, more approachable light. This song is having a similar effect on me. I also think that I may have spotted a winner.

Everyone takes the rest of the afternoon in Symphony Hall at a gallop, running through all the songs for the BBC. Just as the camera rehearsal ends, a distant murmur outside the auditorium has turned into a low roar. A vast audience of families, friends and *Songs of Praise* fans bursts in to create all the atmosphere of the *Last Night of the Proms* and is soon, under conductor Douglas Coombes's direction, in full voice singing the first hymn.

It all seems to be over in a trice, with all six finalists performing to rapturous applause. I glance at the judges, who are nearby, hoping for a clue to the names sealed in the golden envelopes, but they are all poker-faced, giving nothing away. It has all become so exciting that I am later to discover

that all the photographs I have taken are increasingly out of focus as the moment of truth approaches.

'Everyone did wonderfully,' says Malcolm Archer, the judge entrusted with the first cliff-hanging speech, at the end of which he must tell us who has won the prize for *Songs of Praise* Senior School Choir of the Year, 'but the winning choir gave us the tingle factor.'

Clearly he is right, judging by the tumultuous audience reaction when the choir of the King's School, Macclesfield is named. There is much stamping and cheering from the losers too.

My never-to-be-published photographs were taken as Carrie Grant announced the winner of the prize for *Songs of Praise* Junior School Choir of the Year.

'You were all great technically, but it's the passion and enthusiasm of these guys that really communicates,' she says as she draws the winning name – painfully slowly – out of the golden envelope.

There is a terrific roar and even tears of joy when she names Maltman's Green Primary School. Hilary Mason tells me that although the choir had won a competition in the Royal Albert Hall before, this was the first time that they had heard themselves named as winners.

Afterwards, watching the disciplined ranks of children break up into individual, happy mischief-makers and bursting out into the foyer, I am glad that there are no signs of sadness in those who have not come first.

I am a bit puzzled as to why the singing of choirs that I have never seen or heard of before should have made such a deep impression on me. Perhaps it is because they are not old enough to have fallen into the trap of oversweet sentimentality, or the knowing piety that adults sometimes display when singing religious music. Not over earnest, but certainly serious, these young people never hit a false note, and helped make a new date for the *Songs of Praise* calendar.

The King's School, Macclesfield, made their own contribution to Lent by giving their £1,000 prize to students in Africa. With young people like these, we can all have hope for the future.

'The Father's Song', sung by the Maltman's Green Primary School Choir, remains my favourite.

Sing, O Daughter of Zion;
shout aloud, O Israel!
Be glad and rejoice with all your heart.
The Lord your God is with you, he is mighty to save.
He will take great delight in you,
he will quiet you with his love,
he will rejoice over you with singing.

ZEPHANIAH 3:14, 17

I have heard so many songs,
listened to a thousand tongues,
but there is one that sounds above them all.
The Father's song,
the Father's love,
You sung it over me,
and for eternity it's written on my heart.

Heaven's perfect melody,
the Creator's symphony,
You are singing over me
the Father's song.
Heaven's perfect mystery,
the King of Love has sent for me,
and now You're singing over me
the Father's song.

MATT REDMAN

PASSIONTIDE

Christ on the Cross by Francisco de Goya (1746–1828)

chapter five

The Welcome

• • • • • • • • • • • •

When fishes flew and forests walked
And figs grew upon thorn,
Some moment when the moon was blood
Then surely I was born;

With monstrous head and sickening cry
And ears like errant wings,
The devil's walking parody
On all four-footed things.

Fools! For I also had my hour;
One far fierce hour and sweet:
There was a shout about my ears,
And palms before my feet.

'THE DONKEY' BY G.K. CHESTERTON (1872–1936)

Dozens of requests sent to Dame Thora Hird's *Praise Be!* asked to see again the moment from a Wells Cathedral programme when the choirs and congregation sang 'Ride on, ride on in majesty' and a small child perched on a donkey led them all through the Great West door into the nave. *Songs of Praise* may well have set the trend for many more churches to include a real live donkey at their Palm Sunday services. Certainly no one in our own congregation in the medieval parish church of St Mary's Goudhurst in the Weald of Kent could remember a donkey ever before coming into the church on Palm Sunday.

When I married Liz in 1984, among the family I joined were Flicka and Jacko, her two donkeys. Our tolerant and kindly vicar in Goudhurst could see no reason why a little drama was inappropriate on Palm Sunday, so both Flicka and Jacko ambled up the hill to the church in the centre of the village in time for the service. Of course, it could have been a serious biblical error if two donkeys had commemorated the entry into Jerusalem (though it depends how literally you read Matthew's account!) but they were usually inseparable. The vicar chose to begin with numerous lengthy announcements about the Holy Week services and then palm crosses were blessed and distributed to the entire congregation, so the delay proved too much for Jacko, who refused to budge when he got his cue, and Flicka was left to walk up the centre aisle on her own. A friendly and reverent little donkey, she then declined to turn her back on the altar or the vicar and insisted on slowly backing out of the church, even though reversing was not her strong point.

In 1991, when *Songs of Praise*'s rival, *Highway*, commemorated Palm Sunday, Harry Secombe took the road to the New Forest to meet the people of Boldre. As he arrived, Pandora the donkey (who now lives in Scotland) was already on the move into church, accompanied by children from the nearby William Gilpin school waving huge palm branches. Pandora was unflustered even when an exuberant version of 'All glory, laud, and honour' began, accompanied by a Salvation Army band from nearby Boscombe.

As it happened, Boldre was the village where Jacko and Flicka had also been reared, and the church of St John the Baptist, into which Pandora was heading, was where, in the early 1970s, Liz's own Christian faith became real for the first time. She does not remember a donkey coming into church in those days, but every year there was a tradition called 'Gallop to God', when half the congregation rode to Mattins on horseback. She also remembers a wagtail that used to come every spring and tap on the low leaded windows on the south side all through early communion.

Nobody suggested that we find a donkey to come into St James's Piccadilly when President Kenneth Kaunda of Zambia preached at a Palm Sunday service broadcast on BBC television in 1983, although the president, then one of Africa's most distinguished statesmen, would certainly have enjoyed it. He began his sermon by explaining how important the symbolism of waving palms was to him as an African.

'It is our custom, when welcoming visitors, to break off and wave small branches of our trees. Having empty hands is not enough, so we put the branches into the palms of our hands as a sign of deep respect and joy at their arrival.

'Even for us, with our pagan past, we would have cut branches if Jesus had come to our part of Africa.'

He went on to regret that he could only respond to the warm welcome of the congregation of St James's that day with his huge white handkerchief. He waved it and beamed back at their laughter and applause.

'For twenty years, I have been stuck with this handkerchief, as I simply cannot carry some good Zambian branches on my travels round the world.'

Soon we were all wildly waving anything we could find in one of those impromptu moments that so frighten and perplex the nervous television director of a live programme.

With order restored, the president reminded us all how much more significant Palm Sunday was now than it had been on the day Jesus appeared at the gate of Jerusalem riding on an unbroken donkey as a small crowd sang 'Hosanna to the Son of David!'

'Only a few knew then that a saviour had arrived, and now we have the advantage over the few who walked, talked and ate with Jesus. We can look back at 2000 years of history and 2000 years of experience of Jesus at work among us. Christianity ought to be a massive power in the hearts of men and women. But is it?

'Jesus and Jerusalem had no alternative but to comfort each other. How would we face Christ if he came into St James's Church today, or into parliament, or to places of power in Moscow, New York, Beijing or Lusaka?

'Now, as millions of people in the third world are marching into the faith of Jesus, we look to you, the people with such a long Christian history, for the example of Christ's life and love.'

It was 1992, almost ten years later, before I could tell a story for television that perhaps begins to answer some of Dr Kaunda's hard, challenging questions. By then the Berlin Wall had fallen, and in South Africa apartheid was ending. That year I produced a television series for Lent called *People on the Way,* and one Palm Sunday we climbed up from the Rhondda valley in Wales to the hilltop community of Penrhys. With me, apart from the television crew, were Nigel Swinford and his New English orchestra and singers. Nigel has since become a familiar face as a regular conductor on *Songs of Praise,* and he has done much for Christian worship, using both light and serious music.

That Palm Sunday Nigel, his singers and an athletic French horn player sang and played 'Ride on, ride on in majesty' as they climbed the hill. At the top we came to Penrhys Uniting Church, supported by no fewer than eight denominations, which was meeting in a brand new building on the site of a vandalized and abandoned block of maisonettes. Penrhys was built in the 1960s, on a hill above streets of Victorian terraces, and was intended to be a new Jerusalem. We listened to its story.

John Morgans was brought up in the Welsh valleys, under the shadow of a coal tip. 'That artificial mountain owed me six minutes of light every day as it blocked off the morning sun in the Rhondda. One day in 1966, after I had been away at theological college in the USA, I was back in the valley where my great-grandfather had once helped sink the pit, and where he had died in an accident. I climbed to the top of the tip and realized that I was looking down on a community that I wanted to cradle in my hands.'

Years later, John was watching a television programme about the same community. By then the mines had closed and jobs had disappeared. 'It was depicted in a most unfair way, as if everyone was either a criminal or a victim. It was so untrue. I thought, what can I do? I could join them.'

So in 1986, John and his family moved up from the valleys to the hard-pressed community on the hill. 'I moved from living "under the tip" to living "above the tip".'

In the meantime the Revd John Morgans, as he now was, had become president of the Welsh Churches and an influential church leader, but he knew that he wanted to work with the people of Penrhys. In 1991, after two years' work, ten worshippers meeting in a shop had become fifty in the new

church. I believe that both Penrhys and John Morgans followed the example of Christ's life and love that President Kaunda had been looking for ten years earlier.

'It is the people of Penrhys who sustain me, praying day by day in this church, and there are 500 children who come class by class to worship here.'

We also discovered, as we made that Lent series and listened to the story of the hilltop village, that people of many races in the developing world were now travelling to Wales, and many climbed up the hill to share their own stories with the people of Penrhys. As our programme ended, what had at first appeared to be a precarious village on the very edge of civilization and survival now seemed like the centre of the world.

Wisdom unsearchable,
God the invisible,
love indestructible
in frailty appears:
Lord of infinity,
stooping so tenderly,
lifts our humanity
to the heights of his throne.

Oh what a mystery –
meekness and majesty:
bow down and worship
for this is your God,
this is your God.

GRAHAM KENDRICK (b. 1950)

chapter six

Last Supper
in Morecambe

● ● ● ● ● ● ● ● ● ● ● ● ● ●

During supper he took bread, and having said
the blessing he broke it and gave it to them,
with the words: 'Take this; this is my body.'
Then he took a cup, and having offered
thanks to God he gave it to them; and they
all drank from it. And he said to them, 'This
is my blood, the blood of the covenant, shed
for many. Truly I tell you: never again shall I
drink from the fruit of the vine until that day
when I drink it new in the kingdom of God.'

MARK 14:22–25

Suppertime in Morecambe, and on a dull, grey April evening, it was
as if the very buildings and streets were mourning the passing of
the town's First Lady, described as 'a National Treasure'. Just a
few days after Dame Thora Hird's death in her ninety-second year, her
birthplace seemed to be feeling its age, as an unusually bitter breeze
whipped along the deserted sea front. I was on another of my long
journeys, and I had stopped in Morecambe to take a break and pay
my respects.

Although almost ten years had gone by since 'our Thora' had last
taken over *Songs of Praise* for her annual 'favourite hymn' binge, *Praise Be!*,

for many of us she still embodied one of the programme's essential ingredients – cheerful Christianity.

'I'm sad to think there'll be no more Thora,' said the proprietor of the Old Pier bookshop, who keeps a copy of Thora's *Little Book of Bygones* at the cash desk. There on the cover is her smiling face underneath the bright yellow cap that she so often wore on her *Praise Be!* journeys. As he waved it at me, I could almost hear Thora's laugh and her catchphrase 'Happy days!'

There was nothing else by Thora to see in the Old Pier bookshop, because whenever copies of her autobiography do turn up, apparently they are immediately snapped up. However, I had the feeling that if she had been able to pop in during one of her visits to the town, increasingly rare in her last years, she would have been in her element here. Whenever we were together while she and my wife, Liz, were working, first on *Praise Be!* for seventeen years and then on her many books and volumes of autobiography, Thora always enjoyed rummaging through old books and records. The Old Pier bookshop is an Aladdin's cave for anyone who enjoys a rummage. Unlike new-fangled high-street chainstore bookshops of regimented volumes, designer sofas and coffee machines, here was the chance to browse for hours among treasures probably unsorted for decades. In one of a warren of rooms, sounds from an invisible and nearly inaudible radio encouraged me to linger. Was this a time warp, for wasn't that the BBC Light Programme wafting through the shelf of bygone children's encyclopedias?

Although Morecambe was clearly in the middle of a serious makeover, with a smart new arts centre to show off and what must be the world's largest polo mint towering over the promenade, it still retained all the benefit of small family businesses trading from their distinctive seafront premises. I was even able to find a traditional café for supper, where thick slices of bread and butter and a pot of strong tea were an automatic bonus for customers choosing fish and chips.

'Anything more you fancy?' said the flat-capped fellow-diner at the next table, who bore a remarkable resemblance to the late comedian Colin

Crompton. He quickly rose from the table before his wife could respond, adding lugubriously, 'Are you about fit?' They then both began to don many layers of clothing before venturing into an increasingly cold evening. It could have been a scene from one of the Alan Bennett plays that brought Dame Thora international acclaim in her later years.

'All of my life is based on timing' is the inscription on a memorial just across the road from the café. It is not a memorial to Thora, although her own timing was legendary, but to Eric Morecambe, another great television comedy star, and it gave her pleasure to know that her old friend was commemorated on the promenade. 'They'll have to wait until I'm gone before there's anything for me,' she told Roger Royle, presenter of the longest-ever-running religious radio broadcast, *Sunday Half Hour*, who became a very close and faithful friend in her last years.

Now, Thora had gone. Her birthplace and the Royalty Theatre and Opera House next door, where she first appeared on stage as a babe in arms, were long ago demolished. The Central Pier has burnt down and even her favourite Methodist church has closed. Night was falling and the shops were closing, so it seemed best to move on.

I nearly missed God's greatest blessing to Morecambe. I had been wondering in the café why everyone had sat side by side rather than facing each other. The reason is simple: Morecambe has one of the finest views of any English seaside resort. Not only does it face west across a bay over which the summer sun sets, but it also has the backcloth of the mountains of the Lake District. No wonder Thora's father, who managed the Central

Pier for many years, did such a roaring trade in deckchairs. What an experience it must have been, dancing to a live orchestra in the open air with the sea pounding below you, or sitting on a deckchair listening to the band and enjoying this spectacular view – and all for threepence. 'In *old* money,' as Thora would so often remind me.

The view was rapidly vanishing in the darkness as I was leaving, but I caught a brief glimpse of Morecambe's latest attraction, Britain's first hovercraft lifeboat, designed to rescue the many holidaymakers who stubbornly refuse to believe that no one can safely cross the vast sands of the bay, where all Thora's uncles once trawled for shrimps, even at low tide, without a guide.

Continuing on my way, I stopped briefly on the north side of the bay, at Grange-over-Sands, where the two giants of religious broadcasting once met for gentle combat. ITV's *Highway* never quite made it to Morecambe, but Sir Harry Secombe had an assignation with his *Praise Be!* rival at Grange. 'It's over fifty years since I've been on this promenade,' Thora told Harry, as in a stiff sea breeze she held on to her big red hat, a grand alternative to the yellow cap, adding, to reinforce her loyalty to Morecambe, 'We always looked across to Grange.'

Thora recalled the 32 weeks that she and Harry had shared as co-stars at the London Palladium in the 1960s, and there was a little upstaging when the star of *Praise Be!* said, 'Excuse me, I'm not swanking,' and described a fan's recent greeting to her: 'Hello, love, I saw you on *No Highway* on Sunday!' And Harry told her how, on *Highway*, whenever the filming had to be stopped because of the noise of a helicopter flying overhead, he always said to the crew, 'Hallo! There goes Thora in her helicopter, come to spy on us again!'

On Radio 2's special Easter *Sunday Half-Hour*, Roger Royle beautifully captured the spirit of Thora's Christian faith as he remembered their daily conversations shortly before her death. 'God was a mate, sometimes to be told off, but always to be thanked.' And he added, 'Death had lost its sting for Thora, through the love of her parents, her brother Neville and her beloved Scottie.'

The memorial to Eric Morecambe on the promenade in Morecambe speaks of the comic's gift of timing. Once Terry Wogan asked Thora, 'How long do you intend to go on?'

'I'm glad you've asked me that,' she replied, 'because when people don't want me, I shall know. And that's when I'll stop.'

Thora, for once, you got your timing wrong, love. We miss you.

Here is a passage Thora loved and read more than once on *Praise Be!* She also read it to Sir Harry as they stood together by the beach at Grange-over-Sands.

My wife, Liz, with Thora.

Footprints

One night a man had a dream.
He dreamed he was walking along the beach with the Lord.
Across the sky flashed scenes from his life.
For each scene he noticed two sets of footprints in the sand:
one belonging to him, and the other to the Lord.

When the last scene of his life flashed before him,
he looked back at the footprints in the sand.
He noticed that many times along the path of his life
there was only one set of footprints.
He also noticed that it happened
at the very lowest and saddest times of his life.

This really bothered him and he questioned the Lord about it:
'Lord, you said that once I decided to follow you,
you'd walk with me all the way.
But I have noticed that during the most troublesome times in my life
there is only one set of footprints.
I don't understand why when I needed you most you would leave me.'

The Lord replied:
'My son, my precious child,
I love you and I would never leave you.
During your times of trial and suffering,
when you see only one set of footprints,
it was then that I carried you.'

AUTHOR UNKNOWN

chapter seven

Coming Clean

· · · · · · · · · · · ·

It was before the Passover festival, and Jesus knew that his hour had come and that he must leave this world and go to the Father. He had always loved his own who were in the world, and he loved them to the end.

The devil had already put into the mind of Judas son of Simon Iscariot to betray him. During supper, Jesus, well aware that the Father had entrusted everything to him, and that he had come from God and was going back to God, rose from the supper table, took off his outer garment and, taking a towel, tied it round him. Then he poured water into a basin, and began to wash his disciples' feet and to wipe them with the towel.

When he came to Simon Peter, Peter said to him, 'You, Lord, washing my feet?' Jesus replied, 'You do not understand now what I am doing, but one day you will.' Peter said, 'I will never let you wash my feet.' 'If I do not wash you,' Jesus replied, 'you have no part with me.' 'Then, Lord,' said Simon Peter, 'not my feet only; wash my hands and head as well!'

Jesus said to him, 'Anyone who has bathed

needs no further washing; he is clean all over;
and you are clean, though not every one of you.'
He added the words 'not every one of you'
because he knew who was going to betray him.

After washing their feet he put on his garment
and sat down again. 'Do you understand what
I have done for you?' he asked. 'You call me
Teacher and Lord, and rightly so, for that is what
I am. Then if I, your Lord and Teacher, have
washed your feet, you also ought to wash one
another's feet. I have set you an example: you
are to do as I have done for you.'

JOHN 13:1–15

As Edie on *Last of the Summer Wine*, Thora Hird's trick of spreading newspapers out on the floor to stop her husband, Wesley, from dirtying their home with his mucky boots, met with the warm approval of some house-proud viewers, and was nostalgic for many others. 'That's exactly what my old auntie used to do to her husband!' Thora was told by many a fan.

I must confess that I am terribly alarmed if asked to take off my shoes to preserve a pale and pristine carpet when visiting someone's home, because I know I shall almost certainly reveal an odd pair of socks or – worse still – holes. So the prospect of removing my shoes and socks to have my feet washed in front of the whole congregation on Maundy Thursday definitely seemed a step too far. And a bout of uncontrollable ticklish gasps or giggling during one of the most solemn services of the year would probably be the humiliation of a lifetime.

When Rowan Williams decided to wash the feet of the people of

Canterbury on Maundy Thursday as he prepared for his first Easter as archbishop of Canterbury, he was re-enacting Jesus' upside-down view of the world, as described in John's Gospel. In this hierarchical world, today just as in first-century Palestine, in God's eyes the master must be the servant. 'If I do not wash you', Jesus tells Peter, 'you have no part in me.'

I know that I am not alone in often stubbornly refusing to accept help when I most need it.

On Maundy Thursday, as Liz and I travel with some trepidation to a foot-washing service in St Mary's Cathedral, Edinburgh, I am not sure that either of us has really got the message. We have both spent almost the

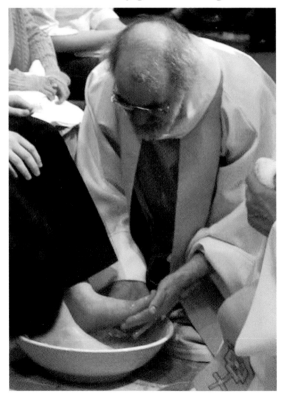

entire day soaking our feet in a soapy bath and there has been much scrubbing, trimming, plucking and application of perfumed unguents. And of course we have selected clean socks that have been carefully examined for holes.

When the moment arrives, we find we are fighting back not embarrassed laughter but tears. Using a large plain china bowl and jug borrowed from the bishop of Edinburgh's kitchen cupboard, Canon Jane Millard, the vice-provost of the cathedral, kneels before her row of 'volunteer disciples', gently bathes our feet in warm water, and then carefully dries them with a warm towel. She makes the sign of the cross on each foot and whispers, 'God bless you'.

I am even a bit tearful as I write about that evening, for this simple moment brought such a huge sense of acceptance and forgiveness. If we British were not such reserved and prissy people, and many still have reservations even about sharing the Peace in church – if the congregation is asked to do no more than greet one other with a friendly handshake – we would surely be queuing far into the night for such an overwhelming and healing experience.

For me, the Maundy Thursday service, more than any other moment in Lent, marks the struggle in all of us who accept the forgiveness of God, but keep falling back into our old, selfish ways. After the foot-washing comes the Last Supper and, as the words of institution say before we share the bread and the wine, this is 'the night when he was betrayed'.

What follows is a small betrayal, but a betrayal all the same. We all help strip back the altar to a bare and abandoned table, and uncharacteristically for a church that values beauty and grace, we deliberately do it in a hurried and disorderly way. This symbolizes that on that night before Gethsemane, Jesus' disciples were edgy and preparing to run away and even deny that they knew him. In silence, the service ends without a closing hymn, and the organ is closed up. Now is the time for the Maundy Watch, but will we stay and pray with Graham and Jane, our priests, remembering the betrayal and arrest that followed?

Matthew's Gospel describes the beginning of the awful night in the garden of Gethsemane. 'Could none of you stay awake with me for one hour?' Jesus says to Peter, James and John when he finds them asleep. Even with our feet and our whole being blessed, the spirit is willing but the flesh is weak and, in the language of *EastEnders*, which we have missed, Liz and I 'do a runner' and drive home. We don't stay and watch, even for one hour.

Drop, drop, slow tears,
and bathe those beauteous feet,
which brought from heaven
the news and Prince of peace.

Cease not, wet eyes,
his mercies to entreat;
to cry for vengeance
sin doth never cease.

In your deep floods,
drown all my faults and fears;
nor let his eye
see sin, but through my tears.

PHINEAS FLETCHER (1582–1650)

A Good Result

Then he came to the disciples and said to them, 'Still asleep? Still resting? The hour has come! The Son of Man is betrayed into the hands of sinners. Up, let us go! The traitor is upon us.'

He was still speaking when Judas, one of the Twelve, appeared, and with him a great crowd armed with swords and cudgels, sent by the chief priests and the elders of the nation. The traitor had given them this sign: 'The one I kiss is your man; seize him.' Going straight up to Jesus he said, 'Hail, Rabbi!' and kissed him. Jesus replied, 'Friend, do what you are here to do.' Then they came forward, seized Jesus, and held him fast.

At that moment one of those with Jesus reached for his sword and drew it, and struck the high priest's servant, cutting off his ear. But Jesus said to him, 'Put up your sword. All who take the sword die by the sword. Do you suppose that I cannot appeal for help to my Father, and at once be sent more than twelve legions of angels? But how then would the scriptures be fulfilled, which say that this must happen?'

Then Jesus spoke to the crowd: 'Do you take me for a bandit, that you have come out with swords and cudgels to arrest me? Day after day I sat teaching in the temple, and you did not lay hands on me. But this has all happened to fulfil what the prophets wrote.'

Then the disciples all deserted him and ran away.

MATTHEW 26:45–56

I have filmed many betrayals and arrests by night for television. In the 1960s my job was to record the successful nabbing of miscreants, because when I first came into television, as a film sound-recordist, I worked through many long nights on Dixon of Dock Green. Jack Warner's George Dixon belonged to a world of bobbies on the beat, petty criminals, tarts with hearts of gold, lost dogs and dodgy car dealers, all forming the back-drop for a weekly detective story which always ended with a reassuring moral message from under the blue lamp.

We always had to film at night, when London streets were deserted and could be lit with huge arc lamps to show Detective Sergeant Andy Crawford, played by Peter Byrne, arriving to 'pursue his enquiries' at a front door, or to show an old-fashioned burglar (frequently played by a now well-known star) lurking in an alleyway. Often a prop telephone box was needed for the action, and invariably a late-night reveller trying to call a minicab would be found wrestling with the wooden replica complete with its dummy phone. Once, an angry resident in a dressing-gown tried to ring the police about the noise we were making, expostulating, 'We've waited years for a phone round here, and now it doesn't even work!'

Just occasionally, the star, PC Dixon himself, would join us (following a tip-off from an old lag who, of course, would talk only to him) to solve a really serious crime. In one particularly dramatic scene, he single-handedly saved a timber yard and a large part of Dock Green from an arsonist. I remember how gamely Jack Warner, in spite of suffering from severe arthritis, playing what must have been the world's oldest policeman, ran to get his man and had a 'good result'.

Mandancin' also had to be filmed at night. It is a newly made, full-length cinema feature by television director, Norman Stone, who has recently produced an edition of *Songs of Praise* for the first time. (His wife, Sally Magnusson, regularly presents the programme, especially when it comes from Scotland.) *Mandancin'* is also about betrayal and arrest – but there its similarity with *Dixon of Dock Green* ends. Norman's film takes up the Passion story in the third millennium. Set mostly at night in modern urban Scotland, the film stars Alex Ferns, who played Trevor, the bête noir of *EastEnders*, and in this plays Jimmy Kerrigan, a hard ex-con. Released from prison, because of the conditions of his parole Jimmy has to become involved with a rather insipid church drama. It ends with him using his own experience of life to transform it into a powerful Passion play. When he has to confront a lethal cocktail of corrupt policemen and drug barons, Jimmy gives the amateur actors his own, hard man's understanding of Jesus' prophetic words in Matthew's Gospel:

'Woe to you,' Jesus tells the teachers of the law and the Pharisees, 'on the outside you appear to people as righteous, but on the inside you are full of hypocrisy and wickedness.'

Shortly before his arrest in the garden darkness of Gethsemane, Jesus tells his disciples to watch out for the thief who comes in the night. To watch and pray.

As a very light sleeper dogged by nightmares since childhood, I dread the night if I'm not preoccupied with making television programmes. Even our own garden, filled with the plants and trees that we have grown ourselves, becomes for me a place of sinister shadows. As the dog urgently insists on being let out to bark furiously at passing cats and hedgehogs, to my anxious imagination the black world beyond the back door could well be another Gethsemane. So night-time filming, or an essential night journey by car, gives me the excuse to avoid tossing and turning in my bed.

One overnight drive turned into a strangely spiritual experience. Moving back to Scotland from Kent some years ago, I had to drive the 450 miles to our new home with Caspar, the cat, and Batty, the dog. We believed the pets would be happier if they could sleep through such a long journey, so I drove them up by night to join Liz, who had set off the previous morning, at our new cottage in Midlothian.

By the time Caspar, Batty and I had finally got our last few possessions together and left, it was midnight, and Batty immediately turned in and began snoring her head off on the back seat. Not so Caspar. He placed himself on top of the back shelf so he could catch my eye every time I looked in the driving mirror. He glared at me, and every time he saw me looking at him, spoke accusingly of my betrayal in taking him away from his home territory. He had a penetrating Burmese voice, so I defended myself with the mellifluous sounds of Radio 2.

We listened to *Pause for Thought*, the short religious reflection on Radio 2 for poor sleepers and night-travellers, first at 1 a.m. and then at 3 a.m.

That helped keep me going, and when I looked in the mirror, Caspar still sternly caught my eye, but silently.

As we journeyed northwards through the small hours, the traffic became lighter and lighter. As the Great North Road emptied, the animal kingdom, invisible by day, gradually took over. Even Caspar began looking at them rather staring than at me. We saw ghostly barn owls, rabbits, weasels, stoats, a snuffling badger and a surprisingly nimble hedgehog, following the ancient paths their ancestors would have known long before the Romans came to Rye or the rolling English drunkard made the rolling English road. We even saw a pair of deer running along the verge before swerving off into the darkness. When I stopped for a break, I dared not get out in a dark lay-by, but Caspar strode forward to climb onto the steering wheel, sensing the excitement of the night. When I switched the headlights back on, I think we were both equally thrilled by the sight of a big red fox in the finest condition calmly loping across the carriageways of the A1. Batty remained deeply asleep.

By the time we crossed the border into a lightly snowing Scotland in the dawn light, Caspar had watched with me all through the night and we had shared the mysterious appearances of the wild creatures. That night, my feline and canine companions had seemed like my guardian angels. Caspar, my extra pair of eyes, and Batty with enough faith to sleep soundly – although she mysteriously awoke exactly a mile before we reached our destination and even sensed which of the car doors would lead her to her new home. Caspar rolled a few times on the carpet, then found a cushion and fell into a forgiving, peaceful sleep himself. While Radio 2's, and later Radio 4's, early morning *Prayer for the Day* had given me hope for our new life ahead, I had also learned that whether or not animals pray, they certainly watch, and they seem to know instinctively about forgiveness. We, meanwhile, have to try to be simply human.

There is a green hill far away,
without a city wall,
where the dear Lord was crucified,
who died to save us all.

We may not know, we cannot tell,
what pains he had to bear,
but we believe it was for us
he hung and suffered there.

CECIL FRANCES ALEXANDER (1818–95)

The Day's Main Story

There were two others with him, criminals who were being led out to execution; and when they reached the place called The Skull, they crucified him there, and the criminals with him, one on his right and the other on his left. Jesus said, 'Father, forgive them; they do not know what they are doing.'

They shared out his clothes by casting lots. The people stood looking on, and their rulers jeered at him: 'He saved others: now let him save himself, if this is God's Messiah, his Chosen.' The soldiers joined in the mockery and came forward offering him sour wine. 'If you are the king of the Jews,' they said, 'save yourself.' There was an inscription above his head which ran: 'This is the king of the Jews.'

One of the criminals hanging there taunted him: 'Are not you the Messiah? Save yourself, and us.' But the other rebuked him: 'Have you no fear of God? You are under the same sentence as he is. In our case it is plain justice; we are paying the price for our misdeeds. But this man has done nothing wrong.' And he said, 'Jesus, remember me when you come to your throne.' Jesus answered, 'Truly

I tell you: today you will be with me in Paradise.'

By now it was about midday and a darkness fell over the whole land, which lasted until three in the afternoon: the sun's light failed. And the curtain of the temple was torn in two. Then Jesus uttered a loud cry and said, 'Father, into your hands I commit my spirit'; and with these words he died. When the centurion saw what had happened, he gave praise to God. 'Beyond all doubt,' he said, 'this man was innocent.'

The crowd who had assembled for the spectacle, when they saw what had happened, went home beating their breasts.

LUKE 23:32–48

In a memorable *Songs of Praise* some years ago, from St Mary's Roman Catholic church in Leyland, Lancashire, some unusual figures featured strongly. These Stations of the Cross, created by the artist Arthur Dooley, depicting the traditional stages of Jesus' trial, crucifixion and burial, are three-dimensional bronze sculptures placed in the arches that separate the congregation in the centre from the circular outer aisle of the church. A visitor looking inwards through the delicate figures in the arches can see the worshipping community gathered around the altar.

Arthur Dooley wrote, 'I began to live with the Man during the two years it took to create the stations. The Stations of the Cross are important to me because in them my personal development as a Christian found its beginning.'

I went to see these stations for myself during Lent. At the fourth

station, 'Jesus meets his mother', I felt I could see that the meeting would have been wordless. Both faces reflect a moment of deep, silent understanding that perhaps only a mother and child can share.

Good Friday afternoon at home in Crichton Collegiate Church, where our small congregation have come to observe the ancient monastic tradition of Tenebrae, meaning Darkness, we are also in silence. Sitting under the immense stone vaulted roof of the medieval chancel, as afternoon turns into evening and then to night, something extraordinary happens. The light of the stained-glass window in the East wall, depicting Jesus praying in the garden of Gethsemane as Judas and the temple guards approach, appears stronger and brighter. It increasingly demands my attention as the interior of the church slowly darkens.

This picture could almost be an image shown on the television news when the newsreader is introducing a look back to the events behind the day's main story. But how and where do people think these particular events began?

The Bible offers four accounts of the crucifixion, written only after the first witnesses had reflected for many years on its meaning. They later shaped their dramatic reconstructions to highlight their different perceptions of how it was terrible – and yet at the same time was the beginning of all their hope. And the artist who created the Crichton East window, this 'freeze frame' of the day's main story, has added his own particular insight. An unearthly angel hovers over Jesus, appearing to comfort him, but everything else in the picture, the countryside around Gethsemane and the approaching crowd coming to seize him, is strangely and disturbingly familiar. You suddenly notice that it is our own, Midlothian countryside: the brook depicted in the window runs outside, just below the west gate of the

church; the trees, rabbits and birds are all natives of Scotland; and the faces in the crowd are the faces of the fathers and grandfathers of our own village community. So we are all there, betraying, denying and running away to watch from a distance. The artist makes us understand that we are all in this story.

What have we learnt about the God of love, and about ourselves, in all of this? And what is our part in the deaths and betrayals that are so often the news main story today?

Earlier on Good Friday, at midday, there is a re-enactment in Edinburgh of the scenes the Stations of the Cross depict, the long walk to the Cross. A quiet suburban street is suddenly thronged with crowds. Police are there to control the traffic as a man, his bare back marked with wounds, carries a large wooden cross up the road. Then he falls heavily, and a roughly dressed man is made to carry it. The crowd, some carrying video cameras, rushes him on, and I, trying to take my own still photographs, miss the moment, in a manse garden that serves as Golgotha, of Jesus' death. For a few moments the traffic is stopped and there is complete silence.

So far, in my own family, I have been spared the pain of watching a life ending in distress. The two people very close to me who I was with at the end both died peacefully, with their youth and beauty mysteriously restored in their last minutes. Only one thing marked the end of life – a sudden stillness, and then a complete absence of sound. It was an eloquent silence – like a last message from the personality I loved, that they were no longer there.

I neither knew, nor knew of, my great-uncle Alan, until recently I came across an envelope in some old family papers, marked with the words 'to be taken great care'. It contained the story of his death in action near Ypres in 1915, shortly after Easter. As a young lieutenant, Alan Coates was leading his men into battle for the first and last time. His story had been written by one of the few who survived the dawn advance.

The words were written to comfort an inconsolable mother, but in every detail they describe events that were not just heroic, but almost 'Christ-like'. And yet I doubt that they are in any way exceptional. Many similar, yellowing accounts are piled up in the archives of the Imperial War Museum, and every year I have heard stories like it told by old soldiers being interviewed on the radio or on *Songs of Praise* for Remembrance Sunday.

'He was not like other officers,' records Sergeant Blake of my great-uncle Alan, 'there was something different… We used to call him "Father"… every single man worshipped him… they all gave him their love.

'He knew all about us, our joys and troubles, for he was always ready to listen and advise. When a man was unwell, it was Lieut. Coates who was bending over him. We are rough soldiers and he kind of softened us… Sometimes he would come and sit with the men, and it was good to see their faces light up, for he was like God to them.'

After having to march 35 miles to Ypres, because transport did not show up, he gave out his scarce officer's rations to the men, who had no provisions at all. Then it seems that he was cold, so his men dug a hole for

him and watched him sleep soundly through the night.

'The order came for the attack. Coates took my arm and said, "Well, Blake, this is what we came for, and here we are! Courage, old chap. It will be a tough job, and few of us will come through, but please God, before they do us in, we'll show them what we're made of!" For a moment he was sad, then he said, "Man, it's rotten not giving us a sporting chance, and it's hard to go." But after that he was joking with one of the men.'

The account goes on to describe how Lieut. Coates fell wounded in no-man's land within seconds of the attack. 'Where is the father?' called out the men. In a flash he was dead. His face was peaceful and serene; there was no outward sign of his wound. He was smiling and clasping the identity disk of another officer. He was buried by his men on the battlefield.

To my modern mind, it is a puzzle that this story was never told in our family. But in past generations, painful stories were often buried under what seems to be a British instinct for reserve. My family, like many others, had signed up to silence as the best healer.

And in silence, a lot of good can happen. As the philosopher Pascal famously wrote, 'All the evils of life have fallen upon us because men will not sit alone quietly in a room.' Our service of Tenebrae in Crichton is coming to a close. As we have sat in stillness, with long silences between the readings and meditations, one by one the candles have been extinguished and we are almost in the dark. Yet still a thin, white light filters through the Gethsemane window, and then briefly it becomes our only light as the final candle is taken away and hidden from view.

The choir under the window sings: '"I am the resurrection and the life," saith the Lord.'

This is the faith that inspired Arthur Dooley, the Lancashire sculptor, to break with the tradition that has the Stations of the Cross end with the laying of Jesus' body in a tomb. Behind the altar of St Mary's, Leyland, in a little chapel, he has made an additional Station, 'Christ rises from the dead'.

As the choir continues singing, 'He that believeth in me, though he were dead, yet shall he live, and whosoever liveth and believeth in me, shall never die,' the last candle reappears, and then we are once again in silence – the silence of hope.

Were you there when God raised him from the dead?
Were you there when God raised him from the dead?
Oh, sometimes it causes me to tremble, tremble, tremble;
Were you there when God raised him from the dead?

AMERICAN TRADITIONAL SPIRITUAL

An Apostle
Trying to Get Out

● ● ● ● ● ● ● ● ● ● ● ● ●

O the deep, deep love of Jesus,
spread His praise from shore to shore!
How He loveth, ever loveth,
changeth never, nevermore!
How He watches o'er His loved ones,
died to call them all His own;
how for them He intercedeth,
watcheth o'er them from the throne!

SAMUEL TREVOR FRANCIS (1834–1925)

O n a sunny, spring Saturday morning in 1981, tourists in Winchester wandering casually in by the west door to the vast Norman nave of the Cathedral of the Holy Trinity and Peter and Paul and St Swithun, were confronted by an alarming and violent scene. Many were rooted to the spot, tears in their eyes, as they recognized an event normally frozen in an oil-painting, a statue – or a crucifix. Under the choir screen, two living figures were already hanging from crosses while, accompanied by sonorous and sinister chords of unseen violins, a thin, blood-stained man was being raised up onto a third wooden cross. It was a shocking scene in a cathedral where not so long before the hymn 'O the deep, deep love of Jesus' had been peacefully sung by a huge congregation for *Songs of Praise*. Now the cathedral was bearing witness to the discomforting reality of the cost of that love.

I don't remember anyone complaining about this moment, which I think would have moved even the most sceptical of agnostics. Had they done so, they would have had to deal with the most unlikely of operatic drama producers, Bishop John V. Taylor of Winchester. Close to the action in his purple stock, one of the Church of England's most senior bishops, script in hand, was supervising every move and line in the final dress rehearsal for the world premiere of *The Challenge of the Passion*, a church opera on an enormous scale. The performance was the culmination of an extraordinary collaboration between Bishop John and the composer, Jonathan Harvey.

My first inkling of what they were planning came on a night-time visit to the cathedral on behalf of the BBC. At the very second that we walked in through the west door, out of the shadows at the far distant end of the huge nave a choir started to sing the *Pange Lingua*, the Good Friday hymn from the sixth century:

Sing, my tongue, the glorious battle,
sing the ending of the fray,
o'er the cross, the victor's trophy,
sound the loud triumphant lay:
tell how Christ, the world's Redeemer,
as a victim won the day.

Just a few moments of this plainsong by the massed ranks of Martin Neary's Waynflete Singers, dressed in black and almost invisible in the immense shadowy nave, was enough to convince the BBC visitors that *The Challenge of the Passion* should be televised.

Before two months of intensive rehearsal for his cast and production team had even begun, the bishop had persuaded Don Sweeney, one of the cathedral choir's lay clerks, to forgo his cassock – and also incidentally his motorcycle outfit – to take on the role of Jesus. The operatic tenor, Brian Burrows, was cast in the role of Pilate, and the two immediately began work on the scene of Jesus' trial, which is at the heart of the opera and makes huge demands on vocal skill as well as acting. We watched the bishop in rehearsal, speaking quietly but very confidently through many tense and complicated preparations. We could have been watching an experienced theatre director of the calibre of Peter Hall or Trevor Nunn. Amazingly, Bishop John, who was approaching retirement, was also coping with cataracts in his eyes and had prepared his script in huge writing with every detail included in a myriad of different colours. I do hope that these scripts survived Bishop John's death, as they were works of art in their own right.

'I think that inside every bishop there is an apostle trying to get out,' said the bishop before the broadcast. 'It sounds very big-headed to say that, and I don't mean that I am apostolic, but what makes the fire in my bones is the longing to make this story more real, credible and valuable.' Although every bishop would probably say 'Amen' to that, I don't think that any other in his position has ever taken on the secular world of television and theatre in quite the same way.

Another great challenge the bishop was to face, at a time of considerable theological debate in the Church, was how he would depict the resurrection. David Jenkins, later bishop of Durham, was already in the firing line of the tabloid press for his liberal views. Hearing about the forthcoming programme, the National Association of Women of Great Britain summoned me to a day conference about the media in Sloane Square. The heart of the event was my attempt to deal with numerous small pink slips handed up from the delegates, almost all of which asked me to confirm that the bishop of Winchester's Jesus would be seen to be physically raised from the dead – and no nonsense, please, to confuse the faithful! So would Bishop John be controversial?

'I don't think it was just inside the minds of the disciples. It was not corporate hallucination. I mean, they were so utterly defeated by the crucifixion. For them, the betrayal of God was even worse than the betrayal of Jesus.

'What on earth can people bring out of such awful despair and the absolute collapse of all their vision and hopes? People get hallucinations when they are high on something, not when they are in despair. So I do believe that something utterly objective happened. I don't know quite what.'

The Challenge of the Passion was shown on BBC ONE on Easter Day, 1982, and viewers saw how the then state-of-the-art theatrical and television lighting technology played its part in visualizing Bishop John's resurrection faith. The lifeless body of Jesus had been placed under the nave altar in the darkness of Good Friday. Then, in a growing golden light, the altar frontal was seen to be transparent, and there was no sign of the body. The tomb was empty. In fact, this transformation was more theatrical than a trick of television, and to this day I do not know exactly how the bishop created this effect in full view of the audience in the cathedral.

When two white-clad angels moved into the golden light as Mary, played by the singer Rosemary Hardy, came to the empty tomb, the church opera could so easily have become a mere tableau. But Bishop John had spent a long time preparing this scene, and the television close-up shots showed a puzzled and then frightened Mary, her tears interrupted by the man she thought was the gardener.

'Woman, why weepest thou?' sang Don Sweeney as the resurrected Christ, and then gently, on an astonishingly sustained note, 'Ma-ary!'

As she replied her amazed 'Rabboni!', her hands reached out to touch the Lord she had almost not recognized. Their outstretched fingers got nearer and nearer to each other, but hesitated and stopped before quite touching. In that unbridgeable gap, the sort where static electricity leaps between bodies, we witnessed the moment in which the Passion story ended and resurrection faith took over. On the close-up television picture it was electrifying. The cathedral audience, even people sitting far away in the back of the nave, said that they had felt the same charge of that moment.

Then a modern-day priest moved across to the empty tomb, the nave altar, and placed on it bread and wine.

'Then they went forth and preached everywhere, confirming the Word, the Lord working with them.'

At which point, the sight and sound of the great cathedral took us over with a great 'Amen' of sound blasted out on euphoniums and trombones by musicians slowly moving down the nave, and an insistent, echoing chime of a bell grew louder as a wash of white light spread right up the Norman pillars and across the roof. In the end the whole church was lit up and we were left to decide what to do with the rest of our lives.

The Paradox

Our death implicit in our birth,
We cease, or cannot be;
And know when we are laid in earth
We perish utterly.

And equally the spirit knows
The indomitable sense
Of immortality, which goes
Against all evidence.

See faith alone, whose hand unlocks
All mystery at a touch,
Embrace the awful Paradox
Nor wonder overmuch.

RUTH PITTER

EASTER

The Resurrection of Christ, Hohenfurth Monastery (c. 1350)

chapter eleven

Easter Day

· · · · · · · · · · · ·

In the morning, when you first awake, say:
'Arise, thou that sleepest; arise, my dull and
drowsy soul, and Christ will give thee light.'

FROM *THE NEW WEEK'S PREPARATION* (1803)

A cold, grey dawn is creeping across the Lammermuir Hills to announce this joyful Eastertide to the people of Midlothian. Most of the dull and drowsy souls are still fast asleep, but our young Burmese cat, Toby, and very ancient hors-d'oeuvre dog, MacBean, rise with the first light, setting off alarms in the garden and disrupting the triumphant dawn chorus, so Liz and I, to our surprise, are up in time for a dawn Easter service organized by our local Church of Scotland parish high on top of Soutra Hill.

As we drive up the steep deserted road with a neighbour, passing only the Sunday newspaper delivery van, other Easter celebrations down below us in nearby Edinburgh will already be well under way. By 5 a.m. in Old St Paul's Episcopal Church, a bundle of specially dried twigs, guaranteed to flame but not to smoke, will have created an Easter fire in the darkened nave, and the lit paschal candle will have been carried in solemn procession to the altar. With the slowly creeping dawn, a wave of 'Jesus Christ is risen today' will already be spreading as shivering choristers, teeth chattering with cold, sing their celebratory anthem in churchyards and gardens all across the city. Before they head for the church hall, tempted by the aroma of hot bacon rolls and coffee, they will be hearing again the life-changing news described in the last chapter of St Matthew's Gospel:

About daybreak on the first day of the week, when the sabbath was over, Mary of Magdala and the other Mary came to look at the grave. Suddenly there was a violent earthquake; an angel of the Lord descended from heaven and came and rolled away the stone, and sat down on it. His face shone like lightning; his garments were white as snow. At the sight of him the guards shook with fear and fell to the ground as though dead.

The angel spoke to the women: 'You,' he said, 'have nothing to fear. I know you are looking for Jesus who was crucified. He is not here; he has been raised, as he said he would be. Come and see the place where he was laid, and then go quickly and tell his disciples: "He has been raised from the dead and is going ahead of you into Galilee; there you will see him." That is what I came to tell you.'

They hurried away from the tomb in awe and great joy, and ran to bring the news to the disciples.

MATTHEW 28:1–8

As our own small band of pilgrims, huddled in the lee of an old stone building on Soutra Hill, listens to the same Easter reading, some sheep, who have been silently champing the coarse hillside grass nearby, suddenly look up and add their own chorus. Any thoughts that they might have understood the message of the angel are quickly dispelled as a shepherd races across the moor, his quad bike loaded with extra food for them and their hungry lambs.

Following a local tradition, we have climbed 1200 feet to the site of what was once one of Scotland's most important Christian hospitals. In 1164, King Malcolm IV of Scotland founded the Hospital of the Holy Trinity for a monastic community to provide relief for pilgrims and shelter for the poor and the afflicted. In medieval times it had the privileges of sanctuary, so once inside its boundaries you were beyond the reach of enemies and of the law. There is even a legend that the wounded and dying of both sides that fought at Bannockburn were brought here.

In the early morning drizzle, in an unforgiving east wind near the iron-gated entrance of the old burial aisle of the monastery church, we are standing in the shelter of all that remains of the once great hospital. Spread across the land where it stood is an enormous wind farm, giant propellers spinning as the wind whips towards us across the bleak moors. It seems a God-forsaken place.

Yet now Soutra Hospital's history is slowly emerging from below the earth. The monastery rubbish pits, which neither medieval looters nor iconoclastic Reformers thought worth plundering, are at last giving up their secrets to archaeologists. Sophisticated third-millennium medical analysis of the debris is providing clues about the origin of diseases, some of which we are still striving to overcome. They are discovering the secrets of the cures, drugs and surgery that once made this bleak landscape a place of hope and healing. It is, after all, a good place to celebrate the resurrection.

In 1977, on the first Easter Sunday *Songs of Praise* to include interviews with local people, we told the story of how uncovering the foundations of another great building had given its congregation new life. Introduced by Michael Barratt, this Easter programme came from All Souls, Langham Place, London, a church that has since hosted many radio and television broadcasts, particularly for many years *The Daily Service* on Radio 4. On *Songs of Praise* that Easter, we learned All Souls' own resurrection story.

On a cramped site, the Robert Adam grade-one-listed church, with its elegant spire, had long needed room to expand. Next door, the BBC's Broadcasting House had already made best use of its own limited space by digging down into its foundations to build underground studios that are in use to this day. What would happen if All Souls too expanded downwards? The architect Robert Potter, a committed member of the church, was certain that All Souls would have been built on firm foundations.

It was an act of faith. In the mid 1970s, the congregation had to raise enormous sums of money to fund the venture, and then hope and pray he was right, as first the pews and then the entire floor were ripped out and mechanical diggers ate their way down into the earth. As they slowly emerged from the rubble, the original foundations were revealed to be a perfect mirror image of the church above, with graceful pillars growing out of elegant inverted brick arches. Buried beneath the streets of London for several centuries, this beautiful space doubled the size of the building at a stroke. With plenty of space now for separate rooms for individual counselling and instruction, or opened up for concerts and meetings, All Souls now had all it needed to carry on and increase its life of Christian ministry and witness in central London.

It was in this same new space, in 1979, that *Songs of Praise* celebrated receiving a special and rare award from the National Viewers' and Listeners' Association founded by Mary Whitehouse. As the series producer at the time, I was proud to receive the award on behalf of the hundreds of people who had helped make *Songs of Praise* over the years, including at least three programmes from All Souls itself, conducted by their energetic and redoubtable choirmaster, Noel Tredinnick. Archbishop Robert Runcie, always a great supporter and friend to the series, was also there to share in the  celebration, and the once dark place hidden beneath the London earth had become part of *Songs of Praise's* own story.

After the cold dawn of Soutra, sitting in a not much warmer St Mary's Episcopal Cathedral in Edinburgh, sunlight streaming through a new window has transformed the hundred-year-old building. With a large congregation on most Sundays, on Easter morning the cathedral is almost full an hour before the service is due to begin, so the welcome stewards are working overtime to find seats for the families and tourists who arrive at the last minute. This year for the first time I envy the ones who are being shown into the Resurrection Chapel which, while appropriate for the day, was always a bit of a gloomy, last chance overflow area. Today the fortunate latecomers sit bathed in sunlight diffused into all the colours of the rainbow as it passes through Eduardo Paolozzi's new south window.

This now world-famous sculptor and artist, born in Edinburgh of Italian parents and educated in both Catholic and Protestant schools, was interned as an enemy alien during the Second World War. He seems to have used all the experience of a lifetime to imagine the resurrection and create this window. Describing Paolozzi's work, the art critic Michael Middleton wrote, 'The core of his art is the transmutation of quite ordinary objects into something strange and compelling and wonderful. It becomes different and newly significant.'

This window is the artist's first attempt to work in stained glass, and because of ill health it is likely to be his last project. In 2002, when the window was dedicated in the presence of HRH Princess Anne, the artist was unable to speak, but he sat quietly in a wheelchair bathed in all the colours of creation that he has used to such effect to communicate resurrection.

Glass fills three tall lancet windows in abstract but angular patterns that London commuters might recognize from the eye-catching decor of Tottenham Court Road tube station. Rather than looking at the sharp-etched colours inside the window itself, your eyes are drawn to normally cold dull stonework, which is transformed into a dancing patchwork of vibrant soft-edged colours as moving clouds cause the sun to appear and disappear. Paolozzi is no traditionalist. He is a man who wants the world to see itself reflected in a new light and be changed.

The light of Easter too is a reflected light. For us there are no torn curtains, no earthquakes, no winged angels with messages. Yet reflected through art and drama and the stories of human experience, our everyday life is transfigured, so that the Easter Day Gospel becomes our own story. It is, as Bishop Richard Holloway calls it, 'a glimpse of the future'.

I danced in the morning when the world was begun,
and I danced in the moon and the stars and the sun,
and I came down from heaven and I danced on the earth,
at Bethlehem I had my birth.

> *Dance, then, wherever you may be,*
> *I am the Lord of the Dance, said he,*
> *and I'll lead you all, wherever you may be,*
> *and I'll lead you all in the Dance, said he.*

I danced on a Friday when the sky turned black –
it's hard to dance with the devil on your back.
They buried my body and they thought I'd gone
but I am the Dance and I still go on.

They cut me down and I leapt up high;
I am the life that'll never, never die;
I'll live in you if you'll live in me –
I am the Lord of the Dance, said he.

SYDNEY CARTER (b. 1915)

Miracle in Presnace

● ● ● ● ● ● ● ● ● ● ● ● ● ●

chapter twelve

Through the night of doubt and sorrow
onward goes the pilgrim band,
singing songs of expectation,
marching to the promised land.

Clear before us through the darkness
gleams and burns the guiding light;
clasping hands with one another,
stepping fearless through the night.

One the light of God's own presence
o'er his ransomed people shed,
chasing far the gloom and terror,
brightening all the path we tread.

B.S. INGEMANN (1789–1862)
TR. SABINE BARING-GOULD (1834–1924) ALTERED

'I am entering a tunnel, so that is the end.'
This apocalyptic-sounding conclusion to a mobile phone call came
from one of the most determined and extraordinary Christians
never to have appeared on *Songs of Praise*. Donald Reeves, retired rector
of St James's Piccadilly in London, had been speaking to one of countless
United Nations officials, European Community bureaucrats and secretaries
to ambassadors as we hurtled through the mountains of Southern Bosnia.
For Donald is on a one-man mission to bring hope to a region of Europe yet

to recover from the ravages of its recent war. On a winding road quite unsuited to the many juggernauts which Adnan, our Muslim guide, was overtaking at death-defying speed, a dark mountain tunnel gave him an excuse to cut off the call before any counter-attack could demand to know why an overworked ambassador should abandon his busy schedule to listen to an Anglican old-age pensioner. Donald turned and grinned wickedly at us on the back seat. On the other end of the call an evasive-sounding apparatchik would have finally got the message, so wittily but ruefully summed up by another British diplomat in Sarajevo, 'With Donald, resistance is futile.'

These days many diplomats, politicians and religious leaders are listening to Donald Reeves, who has marked his retirement from St James's by beginning 'The Soul of Europe', a venture which in his own words is 'impossible but essential'.

I first met Donald at a church service for a conference of religious broadcasters in Sweden, where he surprised and delighted the congregation by striding over to the organ to play a Bach voluntary from memory. And now, whenever he is back at home in England, Donald Reeves allows himself time off from 'The Soul of Europe' for a short time, for a musical pursuit on Sunday evenings involving *Songs of Praise*. It was something I had previously suspected to be no more than a pleasing myth put about by the producers, but with one eye on the TV and a sharp ear for the key, Donald Reeves does sit and accompany the *Songs of Praise* hymns on the Allen computer organ which dominates his living room.

'The Soul of Europe' began with a journey through Europe to see how Christian congregations from its many different countries might work together. Eventually Donald made his way, almost by accident, into Bosnia. He found himself in a country of contrasts. In a beautiful landscape, towns and villages were in ruins. In the former Yugoslavia talented artists, architects and engineers, teachers and business people, women and children, people of different faiths who had once all lived in harmony, were now enemies still traumatized by war, anger and guilt. In one of its most demonic forms, civil war had transformed neighbours into murderers, and in 1995, when the United Nations helped bring the war in Bosnia to an end, there were no winners.

Paradoxically, in a country that had emerged from the Cold War to be part of a modern, secular Europe, churches, monasteries and mosques had all been destroyed. 'The Soul of Europe' has no funds and no political power, but Donald uses one of humankind's simplest and most under-used gifts – listening. He travels backwards and forwards between exhausted and divided people, listening to them each in turn, helping them to find the strength to begin again. As he says, helping rebuild the normal life that most of us take for granted involves more than aid and advice.

Father Zvonko with Donald Reeves

The bridge-building creates those conditions in which the gift of light and warmth can begin to flood into cold darkness. Whenever hands are shaken and fresh beginnings celebrated, however small, these symbolic acts and gestures need to be acknowledged so that they can provide evidence of how the perceptions of adversaries and former enemies are beginning to change. There is no instant forgiveness, peace or reconciliation. As John Milton put it, 'Long is the way and hard, that out of hell leads up to light.'

If the people of Bosnia, who took mutual hatred to such extremes, can show the rest of the world this light and warmth, they will also be providing inspiration for future generations, and far beyond their own frontiers.

FROM *A TENDER BRIDGE* BY DONALD REEVES

Leaving the modern, tidied-up landscape around the city, it was easy to spot the point on our short car journey when we had left Banja Luka and entered Presnace. The car bounced across rusted-up railway tracks where long-abandoned freight wagons and carriages were gradually being engulfed by weeds and trees. We lurched along a road which, unlike streets in Banja Luka, still displayed the destruction of war. Holes left by bullets fired from the hills above had not been filled. Some houses were half-built, others half-destroyed, each in its own patch of rough land. There was a sprinkling of Mercedes saloons and several of those vast four-wheel-drive jeeps that jam suburban streets during school-run time here in Britain. It looked as if anyone who lived here was prepared to leave in a hurry.

We turned up a dusky track and passed some jagged lumps of concrete and twisted steel, then a huge, fast-growing, light-excluding hedge like the ones that feature on *Neighbours from Hell*. We had come to Presnace with Donald to witness a resurrection, in a place that had been almost literally hell.

Early in the morning of 12 May 1995, armed men drove up to the parish priest's house, where Father Filip Lukenda and his youth worker, a nun called Sister Cecilija Grgic, were beginning their day in prayer. Shortly after this, the house was seen to be in flames. As if to ensure clinical dispassion, the forensic expert called to the scene reported his examination of the two charred bodies found inside the house in Latin: *Partes corporis humani in statione carbonificationis. Mors violenta. Homicidium.* (Carbonized human bodies. Violent death. Homicide.) Father Filip was the fifth Roman Catholic priest to die violently in three years. By May 1995, 22,000 Catholics in the immediate area had been forced to leave their homes, and half the churches had been destroyed.

To complete the ethnic cleaning in Presnace, on the following day men arrived at the parish church with explosives, and minutes later the church of St Theresa's was blown to pieces so violently that neighbouring houses were also badly damaged. A Serb military commander later told the bishop

of the diocese, 'We know that churches are the heart of your life and community. If we destroy the heart, your community will be shattered.'

Getting out of the car, we had to clamber across builders' boards in the shadow of a very big, new church. It was only half-built, but was already proof that the Serb commander did not succeed in his aim. As everywhere in Bosnia, we were warmly welcomed. We went inside the repaired clergy house, where a very young Father Zvonko, the new parish priest, took us on his own Via Dolorosa, a short few steps across the hall from his office to the chapel. In the chapel, which had once been the living room and was now full of freshly cut flowers, we sat down in silence while Igor, the new youth worker in the parish, lifted the carpet to reveal the indelible bloodstains beneath. They told us how much the two who died here that day had been loved, especially by the young in the area.

Then Father Zvonko showed us the plans for the new church that was already half-built next to the flattened ruins of the old. Surmounting the belfry, the architect had proposed a sculptured pair of hands in prayer, modelled on 'Father, forgive', the famous woodcut by the artist Albrecht Dürer. The belfry was to be positioned so that at three o'clock on every day that the sun shines in Presnace, these praying hands would create a long and delicate shadow across the place where the old church had stood.

In addition to the work on the church, the young people of Presnace had themselves helped rebuild a new youth centre. Igor showed us round, and then with just pride indicated the huge flight of entrance steps to the church, which he had concreted all on his own in a single day.

Since our visit, Donald Reeves has returned to Presnace to discover that the tower is still incomplete, and in spite of the generosity of a Catholic parish in England, funds for the building work have run out. But now, unexpectedly, Pope John Paul II has announced that he will visit Bosnia, and Donald has been invited to meet him there. He plans to play music for the pope on the last traditional pipe-organ in Bosnia.

The big miracle has already begun, as one by one the dispersed families of Presnace are returning to start again – a new life for the community. It would be another small miracle if work on the tower could be completed and the pilgrim pope could go there on a sunlit afternoon at three o'clock. It would be another milestone on the way for Donald Reeves's 'essential but impossible' task.

Bread. A clear sky. Active peace.
A woman's voice singing somewhere.
The army disbanded.
The harvest abundant. The wound healed.
The child wanted. The prisoner freed.
The body's integrity honoured.
The lover returned. The labour equal,
Fair and valued.
Delight in the challenge for the consensus
To solve problems. No hand raised
In any gesture but greeting.
Secure interiors of heart, home and land.
So firm as to make
Secure borders irrelevant at last.
A humble earthly paradise.

AUTHOR UNKNOWN

The Big Sing

A curious fact that provokes
interesting speculation as to the why
and wherefore of things is that there is
a much greater percentage of married
ladies amongst the contraltos than
among the sopranos. Is it that, as a
class, contraltos are more marriageable
than sopranos, or it is it that their
husbands find it easier to dispense
with their company?

MUSICAL TIMES WRITING ON THE ROYAL CHORAL
SOCIETY IN 1910.

It would seem that the editor of *Songs of Praise*
may have missed an opportunity to clear up this
important mystery, as have I, and all the other
previous editors over its more-than-40-year history. My
own anecdotal evidence is far from scientific, but I do
remember that thirty years ago, when attending the first
rehearsals of the hymn-singing on dark, winter evenings
around an upright piano, married and unmarried, it
was always the contraltos who made up 70 per cent
of the volunteers, followed by 25 per cent of sopranos,
including trebles, while somewhere at the back, were a

mostly grumpy scattering of basses and perhaps one tenor. This producer never asked but always assumed that the husbands would come along when they had finished washing the dishes. There have been many marriages made by *Songs of Praise* over the years, but the tingle factor of the contraltos still remains a mystery.

These days the Royal Albert Hall, the original home of the Royal Choral Society whose marital make-up so aroused the curiosity of the *Musical Times*, has become associated with one of the most popular *Songs of Praise* events. One mention on BBC ONE of *The Big Sing* and the entire hall, with over 7,000 seats, is booked out in less than two hours. Large numbers even volunteer to come along to rehearse for several hours beforehand, learning how to beat the hall's daunting acoustics as they sing the nation's top hymns.

In spite of its association today with great choral singing and with massed Promenaders roaring out 'Jerusalem' on the *Last Night of the Proms*, the Royal Albert Hall was not popular with the critics when it was first opened by Queen Victoria in March 1871. It was described as the 'uninteresting locality' where the queen had to sit through the first and apparently last performance of Sir Michael Costa's *Biblical Cantata*, with a libretto sounding as if it were 'thrown together by accident'.

On the other hand, Victorian 'big sings', large festivals to sing religious choral music and hymns, had already become very popular after the publication of *Hymns Ancient and Modern* in 1861. The music critics were fulsome in their praise of hymn-singing.

'The effect of the whole was most gorgeous,' was how the *Illustrated London News* critic described a festival in Peterborough Cathedral in the spring of 1862, as a choir of no fewer than 1,200 singers from all around the diocese came in to sing the hymn 'Who are these like stars appearing?'. The report added what sounds like a prophetic description of *Songs of Praise*, not due to begin for another 100 years, for the object of the Diocesan Association of Choirs was 'the improvement of congregational singing, as distinct from the prettiness of the small choir, through the use

of broad melody and massive harmony.' A special feature at the festival
and a newsworthy innovation was that 'each hymn tune was played through
before it was sung'!

Another leading article in the *The Illustrated London News* of the day
claimed that the Sacred Harmonic Society's Handel Choral Festival had
come about through the introduction of 'cheap postage, a good railway
system and a huge space', namely the Crystal Palace in South London.
'The practice of part-singing by cultivated amateurs is to be welcomed…
There is nothing more effective to lift the minds of the millions above the
grosser forms of entertainment than the popularization of good music.'

In the machiavellian world of Victorian church politics, familiar to us
from the Barsetshire novels of Anthony Trollope, not everyone agreed that
the loftier purposes of tradition, theology and language were well-served by
encouraging hymn-singing as popular entertainment. As the first edition of
Hymns Ancient and Modern was being prepared, it was suggested that all
hymns must first be translated into Latin verse, as a test for whether they
were good poetry, before being accepted. While it would be absurd today,
although intriguing, to translate Graham Kendrick songs into Latin before
allowing them to be included in *Songs of Praise*, the rapid development
of hymn-singing in the reign of Queen Victoria did coincide with the
rediscovery of hymns in many languages, including classical Latin and
Greek, from both the Medieval and the Early Church. Miss Cox, who
translated the opening hymn in the 1862 Peterborough festival, also left
us the great Easter hymn 'Jesus lives!'

One of the most famous writers and translators was John Mason
Neale, who gave us 'All glory, laud, and honour' for Palm Sunday and
'The day of resurrection' for Easter. He once tricked a friend who had just
written a new hymn. While the friend was out of the room for just a few
minutes, Neale dashed off an impeccable Latin version of the new text.
On his friend's return, he suggested that the words were not new, but from
a long-lost third-century source. Neale's elegant hoax was not appreciated,

however, as his friend was none other than the distinguished poet and writer, but rather serious, John Keble.

Many of the Victorian issues about Christian music still seem familiar to the makers of *Songs of Praise* today, as it makes for its half-century, and 'big sings' remain popular with both participants and viewers. Although I admire what the Victorian writer called 'the prettiness of the small choir', on *Songs of Praise* my vote too goes for the 'big sing'. When the programme came from Wakefield Cathedral in 2003, with choirmaster Jonathan Bielby conducting, the massed singers of the third millennium created all the excitement and atmosphere of any great Victorian music festival. 'How shall I sing that majesty?' the powerful, but once neglected, hymn by the seventeenth-century poet, John Mason, took us to the heights.

How shall I sing that majesty
which angels do admire?
Let dust in dust and silence lie;
sing, sing, ye heavenly choir.
Thousands of thousands stand around
thy throne, O God most high;
ten thousand times ten thousand sound
thy praise; but who am I?

Thy brightness unto them appears,
while I thy footsteps trace;
a sound of God comes to my ears,
but they behold thy face.
They sing, because thou art their Sun;
Lord, send a beam on me;
for where heaven is but once begun
there alleluias be.

How great a being, Lord, is thine,
which doth all beings keep!
Thy knowledge is the only line
to sound so vast a deep.
Thou art a sea without a shore,
a sun without a sphere;
thy time is now and evermore,
thy place is everywhere.

JOHN MASON (1646–94)

For some people, and it would seem
especially for people who live in the
north of England, the best thing in life
is a 'big sing'. Dorothy and Ronnie, two of *Songs of*
Praise's most devoted fans, are stalwart members of the Salvation Army,
where Ronnie plays in the band. They are proud citizens of Oldham in
Lancashire, where, through selling 'The War Cry', Dorothy knows every
pub in town. When I visited their home, I thought I was still in Manchester
but Dorothy assured me I had passed into the Promised Land. 'Oldham
begins at "The Cloggers",' she informed me firmly.

   Their snug home is a *Songs of Praise* researcher's paradise. The walk
to their sofa involves a cautious journey around Dorothy's *Songs of Praise*
archives, neatly stacked in every part of the room: hundreds and hundreds
of carefully labelled audio tapes containing every edition of *Songs of Praise*
and *Sunday Half-Hour* for the last twenty years or more. Then there is
Dorothy's written archive – newspaper cuttings and fact sheets going back
even further.

   I feel sure they would both agree with a fellow northerner, the great
uncle of George Marvill, the *Manchester Guardian* music critic, about the
way hymns should be sung. In 1954, George Marvill wrote about the 'big

sing' in the north, where oratorios like 'Judas Maccabeus' were not just 'grand singing'. He gave us a portrait of his Victorian great-uncle, for whom no performance – even with full orchestra complete with trumpet and drums and 'all t' bag o' tricks' – was acceptable if it began 'without a bit o' reverence'.

Thine be the glory, risen, conquering Son,
endless is the victory thou o'er death hast won;
angels in bright raiment rolled the stone away,
kept the folded grave-clothes where thy body lay.

> *Thine be the glory, risen, conquering Son,*
> *endless is the victory thou o'er death hast won.*

Lo, Jesus meets us, risen from the tomb;
lovingly he greets us, scatters fear and gloom;
let the Church with gladness hymns of triumph sing,
for her Lord now liveth, death hath lost its sting:

No more we doubt thee, glorious Prince of Life;
life is naught without thee: aid us in our strife;
make us more than conquerors through thy deathless love;
bring us safe through Jordan to thy home above:

EDMOND BUDRY (1854–1932)
TR. RICHARD HOYLE (1875–1939)

chapter fourteen

Thorn in the Flesh

● ● ● ● ● ● ● ● ● ● ● ● ●

Saul, still breathing murderous threats against the Lord's disciples, went to the high priest and applied for letters to the synagogues at Damascus authorizing him to arrest any followers of the new way whom he found, men and women, and bring them to Jerusalem. While he was still on the road and nearing Damascus, suddenly a light from the sky flashed all around him. He fell to the ground and heard a voice saying, 'Saul, Saul, why are you persecuting me?' 'Tell me, Lord,' he said, 'who you are.' The voice answered, 'I am Jesus, whom you are persecuting. But now get up and go into the city, and you will be told what you have to do.' Meanwhile the men who were travelling with him stood speechless; they heard the voice but could see no one. Saul got up from the ground, but when he opened his eyes he could not see; they led him by the hand and brought him into Damascus. He was blind for three days, and took no food or drink.

ACTS 9:1–9

I t is odd that the great English cathedral known the world over for its majestic size and beauty is named after a small, unprepossessing, argumentative, middle-eastern world traveller. If we are to believe

Sam Dastor's portrayal of St Paul in the BBC Religion's blockbuster feature, *Paul*, first shown in 2003, this is how the apostle would have struck us. So how at home would he feel in Christopher Wren's great church?

The cathedral itself is the subject of one of the most famous photographs of the Second World War. In black and white starkness, through the smoke and flames of the burning City of London blitzed by enemy bombers, the undamaged dome of St Paul's Cathedral serenely rises. Its survival all through World War II, in spite of being a known enemy target, became a symbol of hope to the nation, because it was almost an unbelievable surprise.

I had often wondered how it had seemed, in full colour as it were, during those frightening nights and days, and thought about the men and women of the emergency services and the volunteer firewatchers on watch night after night to protect it. In the late 1960s I was lucky enough to be part of a BBC film crew that arrived at St Paul's in a London Fire Brigade tender, joined by two powerful fire pumps from a city fire station. Making a documentary about the Fire Service, we had stumbled across a remarkable fireman, Divisional Officer Charles Clisby, who as a junior fireman in the war had played a part in its survival when the air was filled with deadly incendiary bombs. He promised to show us how St Paul's dome was safe as long as there was a fire brigade. To prove it, he would demonstrate how easy it was to train two high-pressure jets of water onto the golden orb and the cross at the top of the dome.

Like many of his colleagues, one of whom we learned had become a Christian after believing that an angel had come to save him as he fell through the floor of a burning building, Charles Clisby knew every nook and cranny of St Paul's. He loved the cathedral and all that it symbolized. As we clambered up past the famous whispering gallery with our film equipment, the fire crews in their heavy boots sprinted nimbly past us. On and on we climbed, slowing almost to a standstill on Christopher Wren's wooden staircases inside the dome itself, until finally we came to a little balcony almost at the top. As every tourist knows, the view from there, even today across a city filled with modern tower blocks, is stupendous. On this spring morning, it was as good as it could be as two huge jets of water arced elegantly across us from below and mostly sprayed the orb above our heads. We got quite wet too.

It was, of course, part of a far more serious exercise. We discovered, as we shared the life of Red Watch at Old Street Fire Station for several weeks, that most fires are unexpected, unpredictable and dangerous beyond words. Cathedrals, as recent fires in York, Coventry and Peterborough have shown, are as much at risk as any other building. But I will always remember the nonchalant Charles Clisby, with his 'I told you I could' smile and water dripping off his officer's cap, as we watched a display that was as beautiful as any ornamental fountain.

Alan Bookbinder, the BBC's head of religion and ethics, has described television broadcasts from St Paul's Cathedral as 'the nation going to church'. The thanksgiving service for the Golden Jubilee of the reign of Her Majesty the Queen in 2002 was a happy celebration, and there have also been national, even international, occasions of sadness, as on the dark, winter Saturday in 1965 when, watched by viewers around the world, the body of Sir Winston Churchill was carried up the nave to the tolling of a great, muffled bell.

On 23 May 1882, *The Globe*, a London

evening paper, had reported the dawn arrival at the cathedral of 'Great Paul'. A crowd of 2,000 were waiting outside, and hundreds thronged the streets from Highgate where, as the reporter wrote,

... he had pitched his camp with a considerable retinue. ... Everyone wanted to be able to say that they had touched 'Great Paul'. Women struggled and scrambled for the privilege, some of them giving a hearty, approving slap, and one little old person, after slapping 'Great Paul', proceeded to give further expression to her feelings by cuffing a policeman's ears. Hundreds of children were helped up to touch, and in some instances children in arms were made to go through the ceremony.

He was not, of course, describing a latter-day mission to London by the great saint. He was describing the last part of a journey from a Midlands foundry, hauled by many steam traction engines, of one of the largest church bells in the world. 'Great Paul' had been accorded the celebrity status now given to footballers and pop stars as it arrived in London's capital. How would the man after whom the magnificent bell was named have felt about the world of modern celebrity?

I do not want anyone to form an estimate of me which goes beyond the evidence of his own eyes and ears. To keep me from being unduly elated by the magnificence of such revelations, I was given a thorn in my flesh, a messenger of Satan sent to buffet me; this was to save me from being unduly elated.

2 CORINTHIANS 12:6b–7

In the BBC's *Paul*, Olympic athlete Jonathan Edwards, himself a celebrity as well as a committed Christian, retraced the saint's footsteps to Damascus and then to Corinth, flitting in and out of the first-century drama as a narrator and honest enquirer. As he stood in the desert above the Damascus Road, Jonathan, who like Paul wants to champion the cause of Jesus of Nazareth, puzzled over the story of Saul. The persecutor of Christians was thrown to the ground, struck blind and terrified by a vision to be transformed into Paul, the chief author of the worldwide Christian Church.

It was fascinating to discover that nothing known to modern medicine or science could provide a better explanation of what happened than the account in Acts. There was speculation that Paul's 'thorn in the flesh' could have been the illness of epilepsy, which might account for him falling to the ground. He might have encountered a fierce lightning storm, or even an earthquake on the road to Damascus. But none of these things explain why the episode created such a profound and total change in him.

Many Christians since Paul have told stories of a precise moment when they became utterly certain of Christ's presence in their lives. Many have done so on *Songs of Praise*. Perhaps for most of us it is not possible to claim a single moment of complete transformation, but looking back on my own experience I can see there have been clear mileposts along the road, beginning with my first heartfelt prayer one morning at school assembly, when I believed for the first time that it would make a difference.

In 2003 Jonathan Edwards also presented a special Eastertide *Songs of Praise* to mark and celebrate the 25th anniversary of Spring Harvest, the Christian festival that has helped draw so many young people into Christian life. On the programme he talked to Jo McAvoy, a young teacher, who described how three years earlier she had come to Spring Harvest for the first time and was wondering how to find something that God would want her to do. She wandered into 'Where House', a display area which helps visitors think about turning their faith into action, and found herself looking at a photo-display of a holistic medicine clinic in Uganda, set up by a mission to HIV/Aids sufferers.

'Do you know, I really think I am going to Uganda,' Jo told the rest of her family. Although she had never been to Africa, or even thought of it, the decision was as firm and clear as it was instantaneous.

Jo told Jonathan about looking after young children whose lives were often so short, and in particular about Joseph, a little four-year-old, who had arrived very sick and shown no interest in his surroundings. His face was empty and he never smiled. Then, 'One day, he reached out his hand, and asked me to read him a story.'

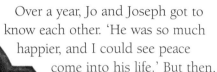

The Conversion of St Paul, Bavarian

Over a year, Jo and Joseph got to know each other. 'He was so much happier, and I could see peace come into his life.' But then, as with so many of the children, Joseph got weaker and died.

'It was deeply upsetting; the little boy who used to come and find me every day wasn't there any more.'

'So where is God who loves the world in this suffering?' Jonathan asked her.

'It's very difficult, but I do believe God does care for us and does love each of us as individuals very much. We cannot praise God for the wars and famine, but we can praise God through it. I've seen children that I've been so close to die in awful circumstances… but God watched his son die so that we could live, so that we could have life today, and that just means everything to me.'

Three times I begged the Lord to rid me of [the thorn in my flesh], but his answer was: 'My grace is all you need; power is most fully seen in weakness.' I am therefore happy to boast of my weaknesses, because then the power of Christ will rest upon me. So I am content with a life of weakness, insult, hardship, persecution, and distress, all for Christ's sake; for when I am weak, then I am strong.

2 CORINTHIANS 12:8–10

Christ, whose glory fills the skies,
Christ, the true, the only light,
Sun of Righteousness, arise,
triumph o'er the shades of night;
Dayspring from on high, be near;
Daystar, in my heart appear.

Dark and cheerless is the morn
unaccompanied by thee;
joyless is the day's return,
till thy mercy's beams I see,
till they inward light impart,
glad my eyes, and warm my heart.

Visit then this soul of mine,
pierce the gloom of sin and grief;
fill me, radiancy divine,
scatter all my unbelief;
more and more thyself display,
shining to the perfect day.

CHARLES WESLEY (1707–88)

chapter fifteen

How Can I Help From Singing?

• • • • • • • • • • • • •

Brother, let me be your servant,
let me be as Christ to you;
pray that I may have the grace to
let you be my servant too.

We are pilgrims on a journey,
and companions on the road;
we are here to help each other
walk the mile and bear the load.

I will hold the Christ-light for you
in the night-time of your fear;
I will hold my hand out to you,
speak the peace you long to hear.

I will weep when you are weeping;
when you laugh I'll laugh with you;
I will share your joy and sorrow
till we've seen this journey through.

When we sing to God in heaven
we shall find such harmony,
born of all we've known together
of Christ's love and agony.

RICHARD GILLARD (b. 1953)

We are singing our *Songs of Praise* in the parish kirk of Edinburgh Castle, the kirk of the Canongate, named after the street that runs along the spine of rock on which the medieval builders built the old town of Edinburgh. The street is part of the Royal Mile, the familiar tourist trail that runs straight down from the castle to the royal palace of Holyrood. It has also been dubbed 'Scotland's bravest street' because so many of the men and boys who were born and grew up here in its once overcrowded tenements went on to fight and die in two world wars.

The long history of the Canongate is as dramatic and colourful as any street in Scotland – sometimes a highly fashionable suburb, sometimes housing the poorest of the poor; sometimes lined with cheering crowds for royal processions, sometimes the centre of turbulent scenes, such as when Bonny Prince Charlie laid siege to the castle from here in 1745. And there are accounts of more domestic scenes of religious divide over the years.

During Lent in 1823, the *Scotsman* reported a sectarian incident that led to an Irishman being taken into custody. It seems that a 'pillar of the church' lived in a flat underneath neighbours whose conduct was described as 'uproarious – and particularly so on Sundays'. There had been frequent quarrels about politics and religion with the same 'pillar of the church' making 'sundry vain attempts to enlighten the minds of his neighbours'. To no avail. One Sunday afternoon, matters came to a head when…

… whilst the complainant was poring over a book, he was in one moment drenched to the skin with a copious discharge of water which proceeded from a hole in the ceiling. He shifted his seat, but into whatever corner of the room he retreated, the cascade followed him and pitched upon his head with as much precision as if it had been endowed with the attribute of intelligence. It was, the 'pillar of the church' thought, 'the offspring of a Popish plot'.

The court's verdict was not reported. Even in 1914, Episcopalians from the nearby Old St Paul's Church were advised by the police that they could not safely make their 'pilgrimage to the cross' in Holy Week because the appearance of white-robed choristers in the 'proud-to-be-Protestant' Canongate would spark off sectarian attacks.

Songs of Praise in many ways marks the healing of a long history of religious division in the Canongate. The overcrowded tenements have gone, and these days the kirk is a place of hospitality to Christians of all denominations, including the many students who come from all over the world to be educated in Scotland. Today's *Songs of Praise* is for school children and students, and is accompanied by the fine new Froebinius organ. It is natural that John Bell, himself a noted hymn-writer, has chosen Richard Gillard's *Servant Song*.

John Bell and the minister of the Canongate, the Revd Charles Robertson, are part of a small team that has undertaken to choose the hymns for the Church of Scotland's new hymnbook. As it is only the fourth

edition to be published since the Reformation 350 years ago, and a tome the size of the Yellow Pages could not accommodate everyone's favourite hymn, they have had to edit their chosen mixture of old and new hymns down to a manageable number. They may well have to launch the new book wearing tin helmets.

Although the politicians in Scotland's new parliament are still concerned about sectarianism in Scotland, the ecumenical *Songs of Praise* in the Canongate now seems a perfectly natural occasion. Denominational differences are hardly ever mentioned on *Songs of Praise* these days, but when the series first began showing people being interviewed in the mid-1970s, it was still thought important for each one to be carefully labelled in the presenter's introductory sentence. This was partly to underline to the audience the fact that the programme was ecumenical – that it was the whole local Christian community, Catholic and Protestant, high and low,

all taking part.

It does seem that the increased coming together of different Christian denominations over the last thirty years has been at least partly influenced by the ease of celebrating faith together in music and song on occasions like *Songs of Praise*. In my own work, since I left the BBC, many of my journeys have been to meetings, retreats and services with even closer co-operation between the churches in mind.

It is only a short journey from our home to St Mary's in Haddington. This historic church, sacked in medieval times by an English army led by the bishop of Durham, is now the focus of an annual ecumenical pilgrimage culminating in a service of healing. Each year there is still always a small group of protesters placard-waving outside. This year they were objecting to the presence of the archbishop of Edinburgh, Keith O'Brien, one of Scotland's most eminent Roman Catholics, and his participation in a service in a Church of Scotland church, and ranting against the man behind the pilgrimage, the earl of Lauderdale. But before the service began, there was a different response from normal. We heard that the old firebrand leader of the protest, Pastor Jack Glass, was unwell, as was his ecumenical sparring partner, Patrick Maitland, earl of Lauderdale. We all prayed together in silence for them both to be healed, before priests and ministers from all denominations began moving around the nave anointing other sick people, many of whom had made long pilgrimages to be together in Haddington on this day.

In spite of producing *Songs of Praise* over three decades, my personal singing career ended with a first voice-test at school, which was mutually embarrassing to singer and examiner. Only hidden well behind a big *Songs of Praise* choir dare I roar and squeak along in praise of God, keeping well clear of the microphones.

Noel Vincent, who also directed many editions of *Songs of Praise* before becoming a canon of Liverpool Anglican cathedral, had a more promising start. He still cherishes his Worcester Cathedral old chorister's prize for 1950, the score of Bach's St Matthew Passion arranged – and autographed – by the great Sir Ivor Atkins, one of the most formidable choirmasters of the 20th century. As a treble in Sir Ivor's choir, Noel once had the painful and difficult task of singing all of Allegri's *Miserere* on his knees, a real Lenten penance, which far from an ancient tradition, was in fact an innovation of his stern Edwardian choir master. What some people perhaps may not realize is that fifty years ago there was as much new Christian music as there is now. Where praise bands and electronic instruments have now become the established way for young Christians to praise God, in 1898 a young Ivor Atkins also joined a new music society, in Worcester, set up by his friend, Edward Elgar, who wanted it 'to do something novel – in fact if they are not disposed to let young England whoop, I shall not take it on!'

Today, in spite of flourishing numbers of girl choristers in cathedrals such as Salisbury and Wakefield, fierce competition to be the BBC Radio 2 Choirgirl and Choirboy of the Year and the annual *Songs of Praise* School Choir of the Year awards, there are still gloom-and-

doom stories in the news about the future, or lack of it, for church choral music. But nurturing musical talent, even in the unlikely surroundings of some of Britain's toughest inner-city schools, is beginning to have results. The future is far more hopeful than is sometimes suggested. There won't be a dramatic, Hollywood-style miracle like in the film *Sister*

Act with Whoopi Goldberg, but the talent is there. As church music evolves with the help of new technology, people like Mervyn Cousins, lately director of music at Liverpool's Metropolitan Roman Catholic cathedral, are, like Elgar 100 years before him, still encouraging a new generation to 'whoop'.

It will need all the patient encouragement that the famous rose-grower featured in a *Songs of Praise* from the Chelsea Flower Show gives to his work. He told us the story of the ten-year process needed to develop the programme's very own variety, the deep red *Songs of Praise* rose, through pollination, growing the seed, then testing and propagation. 'I can put the ingredients together,' said Robert Harkness, 'but God makes the ingredients.' In the dawn of a new day, the new *Songs of Praise* rose blooms for the first time.

Now the green blade riseth from the buried grain,
wheat that in dark earth many days has lain;
love lives again, that with the dead has been:
  Love is come again,
  like wheat that springeth green.

In the grave they laid him, Love whom we had slain,
thinking that never he would wake again,
laid in the earth like grain that sleeps unseen:
  Love is come again,
  like wheat that springeth green.

Forth he came at Easter, like the risen grain,
he that for three days in the grave had lain,
quick from the dead, my risen Lord is seen:
  Love is come again,
  like wheat that springeth green.

When our hearts are wintry, grieving, or in pain,
thy touch can call us back to life again,
fields of our hearts, that dead and bare have been:
  Love is come again,
  like wheat that springeth green.

J.M.C. CRUM (1872–1958)